THE KITCHEN LIBRARY

ONE POT COOKING

THE KITCHEN LIBRARY

ONE POT COOKING

Clare Ferguson

OCTOPUS BOOKS

CONTENTS

NOTES

Standard spoon measurements are used in all recipes
1 tablespoon = one 15 ml spoon
1 teaspoon = one 5 ml spoon
All spoon measures are level.

Fresh herbs are used unless otherwise stated. If unobtainable substitute a bouquet garni of the equivalent dried herbs, or use dried herbs instead but halve the quantities stated.

Use freshly ground black pepper where pepper is specified.

Ovens should be preheated to the specified temperature.

For all recipes, quantities are given in both metric and imperial measures. Follow either set but not a mixture of both, because they are not interchangeable.

Slow cookers, pressure cookers and multi-cookers all vary in design, so it is essential to follow the manufacturer's instructions for your own particular cooker.

This edition published 1986 by
Octopus Books Limited
59 Grosvenor Street, London W1

© Cathay Books 1983
ISBN 0 7064 2980 X

Printed in Hong Kong

INTRODUCTION

Everyday lunches and suppers can tax the ingenuity of the most versatile cook. Providing food for the family seems at times an exacting, slow, expensive and complicated business. But delicious meals need not mean hours spent over the cooker and a mountain of saucepans to wash! The idea of one pot cooking can revitalize the approach to food and liberate you from the kitchen.

It can be very quick *and* very slow; it can be traditional *and* innovative; it can suit novice cooks *and* satisfy gourmet standards; it can be frugal *and* luxurious.

Whether it is a substantial all-vegetable soup, an almost instant fondue, a bubbling rice or pasta dish, an elegant roast for trouble-free entertaining, or an old-fashioned comforting stew with vegetables that you wish to make – it can be done in one pot!

Cooking in One Pot

One pot cooking benefits everyone, not only those with
limited utensils (whether yachtsmen, holiday-makers or
bedsit-dwellers) but all busy people with time, energy and,
sometimes, money at a premium. Selected convenience and
prepared foods, as long as they are combined with a wise
choice of fresh ingredients, can help the process.

Many of the recipes in this book can be cooked in one
heavy-based, lidded, flameproof pan; wherever size or
shape are important, specific details are given.

Certain popular appliances, slow cookers, pressure
cookers and multi-cookers, provide special advantages so a
section each has been devoted to these.

Besides saving energy, one pot cookery can also benefit
health: precious juices, sauces and stocks formed by one
food enhance the nutritive value of those cooked with them
and less goodness is lost. Balance meals by including
seasonal crisp salads as suggested in this book.

Meat these days is expensive, and by no means essential
in family meals; many people welcome good vegetable-
based dishes. These recipes often exploit neglected tastes
and the inclusion of herbs and spices, nuts, seeds and
crunchy toppings can do wonders for jaded appetites.

Many excellent dishes from other countries employ the one pot technique: Chinese stir-frying and layered steaming are legendary; the French marmite or stockpot concept is classic in its simplicity; and hearty Italian meat and pasta filled vegetable soups are timeless. Some one pot dishes are peasant in origin; many more have evolved from the belief that cooking meat, stocks, wine, herbs and vegetables together imparts wonderful richness and savour and has little to do with convenience – though that is a definite bonus for busy cooks.

Relaxed entertaining is easiest if the food can take care of itself, allowing the hostess to be with her guests rather than in the kitchen. Many of the one pot meals in this book can give surprisingly grand results if care is taken in garnishing and presentation. Finger food for starters, and a chilled or frozen dessert to follow – or seasonal fruits and cheese – help make for effortless parties.

Timing in these recipes and the order of cooking should be carefully followed. Once you become accustomed to this convenient way of cooking it will become a way of life.

MONEYWISE MIDWEEK MEALS

Sausage and Vegetable Curry

1 teaspoon oil
500 g (1 lb) pork
  chipolatas
1 tablespoon plain
  flour
2 teaspoons curry
  powder
4 tablespoons tomato
  and chilli chutney
150 ml (¼ pint)
  chicken stock
salt and pepper
113 g (4 oz) frozen
  sliced green beans
227 g (8 oz) frozen
  cauliflower florets
227 g (8 oz) frozen
  sweetcorn

Heat the oil in a large pan, add the sausages and fry until browned; remove.

Add the flour and curry powder to the pan and stir until browned. Stir in the chutney and stock. Add the sausages and salt and pepper to taste. Bring to the boil, cover and simmer for 20 minutes. Add the beans, cauliflower and sweetcorn, bring back to the boil and cook for 10 minutes.

Serve with a rice salad and mango chutney.
Serves 4

Lattice–Topped Fish and Egg Pie

4 cod steaks
1 small leek, very thinly sliced
227 g (8 oz) frozen peas
1 × 376 g (13¼ oz) can tomato and onion Cook-in-Sauce
½ teaspoon Worcestershire sauce
4 hard-boiled eggs
2 tablespoons chopped parsley
750 g (1½ lb) potatoes, boiled
2 tablespoons grated Parmesan cheese

Place the fish, leek and peas in a lightly greased 1.5 litre (2½ pint) shallow ovenproof dish. Cover with the sauces and cook in a preheated moderately hot oven, 190°C (375°F), Gas Mark 5, for 20 minutes.

Cut the eggs into quarters and place on top of the mixture with the yolk uppermost. Sprinkle with the parsley.

Mash the potatoes and mix with the cheese in a basin, then put into a piping bag fitted with a large fluted nozzle and pipe in a lattice pattern on top of the fish mixture. Return to the oven for 20 minutes, until the potatoes are lightly browned.

Serves 4

Stir-Fry Pork

227 g (8 oz) Dutch
  smoked pork
  sausage
3 celery sticks
2 cloves garlic
2.5 cm (1 inch) piece
  root ginger
3 tablespoons oil
1 onion, sliced
350 g (12 oz)
  Chinese leaves,
  cut into 5 mm
  (¼ inch) slices
1 red pepper, cored,
  seeded and cut into
  thin strips
125 g (4 oz)
  broccoli, broken
  into tiny florets
SAUCE:
1 teaspoon cornflour
1 teaspoon sugar
1 tablespoon soy sauce
3 tablespoons water
3 tablespoons dry
  sherry
salt and pepper

Cut the sausage into 3.5 cm (1½ inch) chunks. Cut into halves, then into thin strips. Cut the leaves from the celery with about 2.5 cm (1 inch) celery attached and reserve for garnish. Slice the remaining sticks diagonally. Crush the garlic and shred the root ginger.

Heat the oil in a wok or frying pan, add the garlic, ginger and onion and stir-fry for 30 seconds. Add the celery and stir-fry for 30 seconds, then add the Chinese leaves, sausage, red pepper and broccoli and stir-fry for 1 minute.

Mix the sauce ingredients together, with salt and pepper to taste, stir into the pan and toss the vegetables until a glaze has formed. Garnish with the reserved celery leaves and serve immediately.
Serves 4

Marinated Mackerel

1 dessert apple, cored
  and cut into thin
  rings
625-750 g (1¼-1½ lb)
  smoked mackerel
  fillets
juice of 1 lemon
150 ml (¼ pint) dry
  cider
8 black peppercorns
6 juniper berries,
  lightly crushed
1 small onion, cut
  into rings
125 g (4 oz) seedless
  black grapes

Put the apple in a shallow ovenproof dish. Add the mackerel, flesh side down; make diagonal slashes on the skin side. Add the remaining ingredients, cover and leave for at least 2 hours.

Cook in a preheated moderately hot oven, 190°C (375°F), Gas Mark 5, for 30 minutes.

Serve hot with a potato and lettuce salad.
Serves 4

Cannelloni Florentine

12 cannelloni
1 cucumber
250 g (8 oz) button
  mushrooms,
  quartered

FILLING:
125 g (4 oz) ham,
  diced
227 g (8 oz) frozen
  chopped spinach,
  thawed
2 tablespoons grated
  Parmesan cheese
grated nutmeg
salt and pepper

SAUCE:
2 cloves garlic,
  crushed
1 × 540 ml (19 fl oz)
  can tomato juice
1 bay leaf
1 tablespoon lemon
  juice
few dashes of
  Worcestershire and
  Tabasco sauces

TOPPING:
5 slices processed
  Cheddar cheese

Mix the filling ingredients together, seasoning with nutmeg, salt and pepper to taste, and use to fill the cannelloni.

Mix together the sauce ingredients, adding salt and pepper to taste. Pour a little sauce into an ovenproof dish large enough to take the cannelloni in a single layer. Place the cannelloni on top and pour over the remaining sauce. Cut the cucumber into 1 cm (½ inch) slices, then into quarters. Arrange along each side of the cannelloni with the mushrooms.

Cover with foil and bake in a preheated hot oven, 220°C (425°F), Gas Mark 7, for 30 minutes. Remove the bay leaf.

Cut the cheese into thin strips, sprinkle on top of the cannelloni and return to the oven for 10 minutes, until golden.

Serve with a green salad.

Serves 4

Frypan Pizza

1 × 142 g (5 oz)
  packet instant
  potato
1 tablespoon dried
  onion
450 ml (¾ pint)
  boiling water
2 eggs
2 tablespoons plain
  flour
15 g (½ oz) butter
1 tablespoon oil
1 × 215 g (7.58 oz)
  can tomato and herb
  pizza topping
2 cloves garlic,
  chopped
3 tomatoes, cut into
  thin segments
50 g (2 oz) peperami
1 tablespoon capers
salt and pepper
50 g (2 oz) matured
  Cheddar cheese
½ teaspoon dried
  oregano
TO GARNISH:
black olives
thin onion rings
parsley sprig

Put the potato powder and onion
into a basin. Pour on the boiling
water and stir with a fork. Quickly
stir in one egg at a time and then the
flour to make a thick, smooth
mixture.

Melt the butter and oil in a 23 cm
(9 inch) heavy-based frying pan, add
the potato mixture and smooth to
make an even layer. Cook over a low
heat for 5 minutes, then place under
a preheated hot grill, 5 to 7.5 cm (2 to
3 inches) from heat, for 5 minutes or
until the top begins to brown.

Quickly spread with the pizza
topping and sprinkle with the garlic.
Arrange the tomato in a circle
around the edge. Cut the peperami in
half crossways then lengthways and
arrange like the spokes of a wheel.
Sprinkle with the capers, and salt and
pepper to taste.

Slice the cheese thinly and place
between the peperami. Sprinkle with
the oregano. Return to the grill until
the cheese is bubbling.

Garnish with olives, onions and
parsley and serve immediately, with
a green salad.
Serves 4 to 6

Florida Chicken Drumsticks

2 tablespoons oil
8 chicken drumsticks
1 × 600 ml (1 pint)
    packet asparagus
    soup mix
300 ml (½ pint)
    boiling water
1 small onion, cut
    into 8 pieces
227 g (8 oz) frozen
    cut green beans
salt and pepper
TO GARNISH:
1 avocado
1 × 25 g (1 oz)
    packet potato
    crisps, crushed

Heat the oil in a large pan, add the drumsticks and fry until brown on both sides. Sprinkle in the soup mix, stir in the boiling water and add the onion. Cook over a moderate heat, turning the chicken occasionally, for about 3 to 4 minutes, until a sauce is formed.

Stir in the beans and season to taste with salt and pepper. Cover and simmer for 30 minutes or until the chicken is tender.

Cut the avocado into 12 segments and arrange them over the chicken. Cover and heat through for about 2 to 3 minutes.

Sprinkle with the crushed crisps and serve immediately, with a carrot, cucumber and potato salad.
Serves 4

Salami-Stuffed Tomatoes

4 very large tomatoes
1 tablespoon oil
15 g (½ oz) butter
350 g (12 oz)
    potatoes, sliced
1 clove garlic,
    chopped
142 ml (5 fl oz)
    soured cream
salt and pepper
125 g (4 oz) Danish
    salami
2 pickled sour-sweet
    cucumbers,
    chopped
75 g (3 oz) matured
    Cheddar cheese,
    diced
75 g (3 oz) bread,
    crust removed,
    diced
3 tablespoons
    cucumber relish

Cut the tomatoes in half, remove seeds and core and invert to drain.

Heat the oil and butter in a wide flameproof casserole, add the potatoes and garlic and fry gently until the potatoes are just beginning to brown. Add all but 2 tablespoons of the cream, and salt and pepper to taste. Cover and simmer for 10 minutes.

Reserve 4 slices of salami. Cut the rest into strips and mix with the cucumber and cheese. Add the bread, relish, and salt and pepper. Divide between the tomato halves and place on the potatoes. Cover and cook in a preheated moderately hot oven, 200°C (400°F), Gas Mark 6, for 20 minutes.

Garnish each tomato half with a half slice of salami and pour on a little cream. Serve with a green salad.
Serves 4

Slimmers' Ham Rolls

1 × 326 g (11½ oz)
  can sweetcorn,
  drained
16 leaves chicory
8 long slices cooked
  ham
227 g (8 oz) cottage
  cheese with chives
SAUCE:
1 tablespoon lemon
  juice
1 tablespoon water
1 tablespoon made
  mustard
1 tablespoon
  mayonnaise
2 tablespoons
  hamburger relish

TO GARNISH:
chopped chives

Put the sweetcorn in a shallow ovenproof dish. Put the chicory leaves together in pairs. Do not separate the ham slices – put a pair of leaves at one end on the top slice. Fill the leaves with some of the cottage cheese and roll up in the slice of ham. Place on top of the sweetcorn. Repeat with the remaining ham, chicory and cottage cheese until 8 rolls have been made.

Mix the sauce ingredients together and pour over the ham. Cook in a preheated moderately hot oven, 190°C (375°F), Gas Mark 5, for 15 to 20 minutes. Garnish with chives. Serve with a mixed salad.
Serves 4

Turkey and Bacon Brochettes

2 × 227 g (8 oz)
   cartons turkey
   livers
14 rashers smoked
   streaky bacon,
   derinded and
   halved
1 tablespoon oil
125 g (4 oz) carrots,
   cut into matchstick
   strips
1 onion, cut into
   matchstick strips
600 ml (1 pint)
   water
1 chicken stock cube
juice of ½ lemon
salt and pepper
250 g (8 oz)
   quick-cook
   macaroni
1 large green pepper,
   cored and seeded
1 tablespoon chopped
   parsley

Cut the livers into 28 pieces. Wrap the bacon around the livers and thread on four 18 cm (7 inch) skewers.

Heat the oil in a large flameproof casserole, add the brochettes and fry for 1 minute on each side, turning carefully; remove.

Add the carrots and onion to the pan and stir-fry for 2 minutes. Add the water, stock cube, lemon juice, and salt and pepper to taste and bring to the boil. Stir in the macaroni, bring back to the boil and place the brochettes on top. Cover and cook just at boiling point for 12 minutes.

Cut 8 thin rings from the pepper and keep on one side for garnish. Dice the rest and add to the pan. Cover and leave for a few minutes, off the heat, until the moisture is absorbed.

Transfer the macaroni to a warmed serving dish and arrange the brochettes on top. Garnish with the pepper rings and parsley.
Serves 4

Hawaiian Frankfurters

2 tablespoons oil
1 onion, sliced
125 g (4 oz)
    courgettes, cut into
    thin strips
50 g (2 oz) small
    French beans
25 g (1 oz) stem
    ginger, sliced
1 × 439 g (15½ oz)
    can pineapple
    slices in natural
    juice
2 teaspoons soy sauce
salt and pepper
125 g (4 oz) egg
    noodles, broken
    into small pieces
3 × 170 g (6 oz)
    packs continental
    frankfurters
chopped green pepper
    to garnish

Heat the oil in a large shallow pan, add the onion and fry until lightly browned. Add the courgettes and cook for a few minutes to soften. Stir in the beans and ginger.

Drain the juice from the pineapple, add the soy sauce and make up to 450 ml (¾ pint) with water. Season lightly with salt and pepper. Add to the pan and stir in the noodles. Cover and bring to the boil. Score diagonally along one side of the frankfurters and place on the vegetables.

Bring back to the boil, cover and simmer for 25 minutes. Stir well, put the pineapple on top, cover and heat through for 5 minutes.

Serve hot, garnished with green pepper.
Serves 4

Tuscany Soup

250 g (8 oz) chick
  peas
1.2 litres (2 pints)
  chicken stock
600 ml (1 pint) dry
  white wine or
  cider
1 onion, studded
  with 2 cloves
3 cloves garlic,
  crushed
2-3 rosemary sprigs
2 bay leaves
good pinch of
  powdered saffron
250 g (8 oz) streaky
  pork, sliced
750 g (1½ lb)
  chicken wings
25 g (1 oz) noodles
salt and white pepper
250 g (8 oz) spinach
  leaves

Put the chick peas in a large pan and cover with cold water. Bring to the boil and boil for 10 minutes. Turn off the heat, cover the pan and leave for 1 hour.

Drain off the water. Add the chicken stock, wine or cider, onion, garlic, rosemary, bay leaves, saffron, pork and chicken wings to the peas in the pan. Bring to the boil, cover and simmer for 1½ hours. Remove the onion, rosemary and bay leaves.

Add the noodles, and salt and pepper to taste and cook for 10 minutes. Add the spinach and simmer for 5 minutes. Adjust the seasoning.

Serve with crusty bread or rolls.
Serves 6 to 8

Traditional Lancashire Hotpot

1 kg (2 lb) potatoes
500 g (1 lb) scrag
   and middle neck
   lamb
125 g (4 oz) lambs'
   kidneys, skinned,
   halved and cored
1 large onion, sliced
1 large carrot, sliced
salt and pepper
300 ml (½ pint)
   boiling water
15 g (½ oz)
   margarine or
   dripping, melted
parsley sprig to
   garnish

Grease a 1.5 litre (2½ pint) deep casserole. Halve enough potatoes to cover the top of the dish and set aside. Slice the rest thickly and put in the casserole. Cover with the lamb, kidneys, onion and carrot, seasoning each layer with salt and pepper to taste. Pour in the boiling water. Cover with the reserved potatoes and brush with the melted fat.

Cover and cook in a preheated moderately hot oven, 190°C (375°F), Gas Mark 5, for 2 hours, removing the lid after 1 hour to brown the potatoes. Garnish with parsley.

Serve with a green bean salad.
Serves 4

Cheat's Chicken and Ham Pie

350 g (12 oz) cooked
  chicken, cut into
  pieces
250 g (8 oz) cooked
  ham or bacon, cubed
1 × 600 ml (1 pint)
  packet chicken
  noodle soup mix
125 g (4 oz) mush-
  rooms, quartered
125 g (4 oz) red
  pepper, cored,
  seeded and diced
125 g (4 oz) leek,
  thinly sliced
white pepper
300 ml (½ pint)
  boiling water
1 × 215 g (7½ oz)
  packet frozen puff
  pastry, thawed
beaten egg to glaze
parsley sprigs to
  garnish

Put the chicken, ham or bacon and soup mix in an oval 1.2 litre (2 pint) ovenproof pie dish and mix together well. Add the mushrooms, red pepper, leek, and pepper to taste. Pour in the water.

Roll out the pastry to a 25 cm (10 inch) square and cut out 15 rounds with a 5 cm (2 inch) fluted cutter. Arrange them overlapping around the edge of the dish and in a line down the centre. Brush with beaten egg.

Cook in a preheated hot oven, 230°C (450°F), Gas Mark 8, for 15 minutes, then lower the heat to 190°C (375°F), Gas Mark 5, and cook for a further 10 minutes.

Garnish with parsley and serve with a green salad.
Serves 4

Aubergine and Bean Bake

2 tablespoons oil
250 g (8 oz)
    aubergine,
1 × 447 g (15¾ oz)
    can baked beans
1 tablespoon hot
    pepper sauce
227 g (8 oz) frozen
    sliced green beans
1 × 425 g (15 oz)
    can butter beans
250 g (8 oz) tomatoes,
    thinly sliced
¼ teaspoon dried thyme
2 tablespoons
    chopped parsley
salt and pepper
50 g (2 oz) Cheddar
    cheese

Heat the oil in a 1.5 litre (2½ pint) flameproof casserole. Cut the aubergine into 1 cm (½ inch) cubes and fry for 6 to 8 minutes; remove. · Pour the baked beans and pepper sauce into the casserole, off the heat. Cover with the green beans, then the drained butter beans and spread the aubergine evenly on top. Arrange the tomato in circles from the centre, leaving a border. Sprinkle with the thyme, parsley, and salt and pepper to taste.

Slice the cheese very thinly, then cut into triangles. Arrange on top, overlapping the tomato.

Cook in a preheated moderately hot oven, 200°C (400°F), Gas Mark 6, for 30 minutes. Serve hot.
Serves 4

Fruity Tongue Casserole

25 g (1 oz) butter
15 g (½ oz) plain
    flour
1 × 411 g (14½ oz)
    can apricot halves
grated rind and juice
    of ¼ orange
1 teaspoon Worcester-
    shire sauce
50 g (2 oz) raisins
4 × 177 g (6 oz)
    cans lunch tongue
50 g (2 oz) celery,
    chopped
1 onion, chopped
1 × 539 g (1 lb 3 oz)
    can sliced new
    potatoes, drained
½ teaspoon poppy
    seeds
salt and pepper
parsley sprig to
    garnish

Melt half the butter in a 1.2 litre (2 pint) flameproof casserole. Stir in the flour, half the apricot syrup, the orange rind and juice and Worcestershire sauce to make a smooth sauce. Stir in the raisins.

Cut the apricot halves in half and cut each can of tongue into 4 slices. Put half the apricots in the casserole and cover with half the tongue, celery and onion; repeat the layers.

Arrange the potato on top and sprinkle with the poppy seeds, and salt and pepper to taste. Dot with the remaining butter.

Cook in a preheated moderately hot oven, 200°C (400°F), Gas Mark 6, for 30 minutes, until hot. Increase heat to 230°C (450°F), Gas Mark 8, and cook for 10 minutes, until browned. Garnish with parsley.
Serves 4

French-Style Risotto

1 fennel bulb
2 tablespoons oil
25 g (1 oz) butter
1 bunch spring onions
2 cloves garlic
250 g (8 oz)
    long-grain rice
200 g (7 oz) French
    garlic sausage,
    sliced diagonally
4 cabanos, sliced
750 ml (1¼ pints)
    chicken stock
1 × 62 g (2.2 oz)
    packet quick-dried
    peas
3 tablespoons
    chopped parsley
salt and pepper
shredded rind of
    1 lemon
2 tablespoons
    mayonnaise
1 tablespoon chopped
    basil
basil sprig to garnish

Slice the fennel, reserving the leaves.

Heat the oil and butter in a heavy-based pan. Reserve two of the onions for garnish and chop the rest. Chop the garlic. Add the chopped onions and garlic to the fat with the rice. Stir until the rice grains are coated with fat and lightly coloured.

Stir in the fennel, garlic sausage, cabanos and stock. Bring to the boil and add the peas, 1 tablespoon of the parsley, and salt and pepper to taste. Cover and simmer for 15 minutes or until all the moisture has been absorbed.

Stir in the lemon rind and mayonnaise and sprinkle with the basil, remaining parsley and reserved fennel leaves. Garnish with the reserved onions and basil and serve immediately.
Serves 4

Stuffed Pork Chops with Parsley Dumplings

4 pork chops
75 g (3 oz)
  Emmental cheese,
  sliced
8 sage leaves or ½
  teaspoon dried sage
2 tablespoons oil
2 onions, sliced
1 dessert apple,
  cored
salt and pepper
600 ml (1 pint) dry
  cider
227 g (8 oz) frozen
  broad beans
DUMPLINGS:
125 g (4 oz)
  self-raising flour
pinch of salt
25 g (1 oz) butter
1 teaspoon paprika
4 tablespoons
  chopped parsley
4 tablespoons water

Cut a pocket in the flesh of the pork chops and put a quarter of the cheese and sage into each. Heat the oil in a flameproof casserole, add the chops and onions and fry until lightly browned.

Cut the apple into 8 slices. Place 2 slices on each chop and sprinkle lightly with salt and pepper. Pour in the cider, bring to the boil and simmer for 30 minutes.

Meanwhile, make the dumplings. Sift the flour and salt into a bowl. Rub in the butter until the mixture resembles breadcrumbs. Stir in the paprika and parsley. Add the water and mix to a soft dough. Knead lightly and form into 16 small dumplings. Add to the pan with the broad beans, cover and simmer for 15 minutes. Serve hot.
Serves 4

MEALS WITHOUT MEAT

West Indian Okra with Prawns

500 g (1 lb) okra
2 tablespoons oil
1 large onion,
  chopped
1 large clove garlic,
  chopped
350 g (12 oz) small
  potatoes, cut in
  quarters lengthways
1 × 397 g (14 oz)
  can tomatoes
¼ teaspoon chilli
  powder
¾ teaspoon ground
  cumin
1 bay leaf
salt and pepper
227 g (8 oz) frozen
  peeled prawns,
  thawed

Trim off the brown ends of the okra stalks only; if too much is trimmed off and the insides and seeds of the okra are exposed, the consistency of this dish will be spoilt and the juice and flavour will escape.

Heat the oil in a pan, add the onion and garlic and fry until softened. Add the okra, potatoes, tomatoes with their juice, chilli powder, cumin, bay leaf, and salt and pepper to taste. Bring to the boil, cover and simmer for 30 minutes. Stir in the prawns, cover and cook for 3 minutes, or until the prawns are heated through. Discard the bay leaf.

Serves 4

Leek and Egg Flan

1 × 215 g (7½ oz)
    packet frozen
    shortcrust pastry,
    thawed
175 g (6 oz) leeks,
    very thinly sliced
142 ml (5 fl oz)
    soured cream
salt and pepper
4 eggs
4 anchovy fillets,
    halved
parsley sprigs to
    garnish

Roll out the pastry and use to line a 20 cm (8 inch) flan ring or tin. Line with greaseproof paper and dried beans and 'bake blind' in a preheated moderately hot oven, 200°C (400°F), Gas Mark 6, for 10 minutes. Remove the beans and paper and return to the oven for 5 minutes.

Put the leeks in the pastry case, spread the cream evenly on top and sprinkle with salt and pepper. Return to the oven for 15 minutes.

Make 4 deep depressions in the flan, using the back of a tablespoon, and break an egg into each. Lay the anchovy fillets across the eggs and sprinkle with pepper.

Return to the oven for 10 to 15 minutes, until the eggs are lightly set. Garnish with parsley and serve with tomato halves.
Serves 4

Hearty Pumpkin Soup

750 g (1½ lb)
  pumpkin, diced
1 onion, chopped
50 g (2 oz) brown
  rice
500 g (1 lb) carrots,
  sliced lengthways
1.2 litres (2 pints)
  boiling chicken
  stock
¼ teaspoon ground
  nutmeg
10 cm (4 inch) stick
  cinnamon, halved
¼ teaspoon ground
  mixed spice
salt and pepper
113 g (4 oz) frozen
  peas
1 orange to garnish

Place the pumpkin, onion, rice, carrots and boiling stock in a large pan. Add the spices, and salt and pepper to taste and simmer for about 45 minutes, until the rice is soft. Add the peas and cook for 5 minutes. Discard the cinnamon stick.

Cut 4 thin slices from the centre of the orange for garnish. Grate the rest of the rind and squeeze out the juice. Stir the grated rind and juice into the soup. Serve in individual soup bowls, garnished with a twisted orange slice.

Serve with wholewheat bread and parsley butter.
Serves 4

Braised Leeks

500 g (1 lb) baby
  leeks
1 dessert apple,
  peeled, cored and
  cut into 8 pieces
1 × 439 g (15½ oz)
  can red kidney
  beans, drained
1 clove garlic, crushed
SAUCE:
1 × 64 g (2¼ oz)
  can tomato purée
2 tablespoons oil
½ teaspoon ground
  coriander
150 ml (¼ pint) hot
  water
2 tablespoons white
  wine or stock
salt and pepper
TO GARNISH:
coriander or parsley
  leaves

Put the leeks in a large flameproof casserole. Add the apple, beans and garlic.

Mix the sauce ingredients together, seasoning with salt and pepper to taste, and pour into the casserole. Cover and cook gently for 20 to 25 minutes, until the leeks are just tender.

Garnish with coriander or parsley and serve hot.
Serves 4

Vegetable Moussaka

250 g (8 oz) courgettes
250 g (8 oz)
  aubergine, cubed
salt and pepper
¼ teaspoon ground
  oregano
350 g (12 oz)
  potatoes
1 large onion, sliced
SAUCE:
2 tablespoons tomato
  purée
1 tablespoon olive oil
2 cloves garlic,
  crushed
grated rind and juice
  of ½ lemon
300 ml (½ pint)
  vegetable stock
TOPPING:
150 g (5.2 oz)
  natural yogurt
1 egg, beaten
50 g (2 oz) Cheddar
  cheese, grated
TO GARNISH:
parsley sprig

Cut the courgettes in half crossways, then lengthways into sticks. Place the aubergine in a lightly greased 1.75 litre (3 pint) deep casserole and sprinkle lightly with salt and pepper. Cover with the courgettes and sprinkle with the oregano and a little salt and pepper. Thickly slice the potatoes and arrange half on top of the courgettes. Cover with the onion, then the remaining potatoes, seasoning each layer with salt and pepper to taste.

Mix the sauce ingredients together and pour into the casserole. Cover and cook in a preheated moderate oven, 180°C (350°F), Gas Mark 4, for 1 hour.

Mix the topping ingredients together, pour over the potatoes and return to the oven for 30 minutes, until golden brown. Garnish with parsley and serve with crusty rolls.
Serves 4

Mushroom Layer Loaf

125 g (4 oz) button
  mushrooms, sliced
50 g (2 oz) butter
2 tablespoons
  chopped parsley
6 slices stale bread,
  crusts removed
350 g (12 oz) flat
  mushrooms,
  chopped
250 g (8 oz) fresh
  white breadcrumbs
1 egg, beaten
1 teaspoon yeast
  extract, dissolved
  in a little boiling
  water
salt and pepper
8 tomatoes
SAUCE:
½ × 150 g (5.2 oz)
  carton natural
  yogurt
½ × 142 ml (5 fl oz)
  carton soured
  cream
grated rind of
  ½ lemon
1 teaspoon paprika

Grease a 1 kg (2 lb) loaf tin and line with foil, leaving enough to cover the top later. Grease the foil.

Arrange half the sliced mushrooms down centre of tin. Mix butter and parsley and spread on the bread.

Mix the chopped mushrooms, breadcrumbs, egg and yeast extract together with salt and pepper to taste.

Arrange half the bread slices, overlapping, buttered side down on the mushroom slices, and cover with half the chopped mushroom mixture, pressing well down. Cover with the remaining sliced mushrooms, then the remaining mushroom mixture. Finish with the remaining bread and bring the foil over the top.

Place in a roasting pan. Pour in boiling water to a depth of 1 cm (½ inch). Cook in a preheated moderately hot oven, 190°C (375°F), Gas Mark 5, for 30 minutes. Open the foil. Cut a cross on each tomato and place around the loaf in the roasting pan. Cook for 15 minutes. Mix together the sauce ingredients. Serve the loaf and tomatoes with the sauce, and a butter bean and watercress salad.
Serves 4

Sweet Potato Patties

750 g (1½ lb) sweet
potato, cut into 1 cm
(½ inch) cubes
salt and pepper
1 tablespoon soft
light brown sugar
1½ teaspoons ground
cardamom
75 g (3 oz) cornflakes,
crushed
4 tablespoons oil
450 ml (¾ pint) dry
cider
2 celery sticks, finely
sliced
50 g (2 oz) broccoli,
broken into very
small florets
2 teaspoons plain
flour
15 g (½ oz) butter

Cook the sweet potato in boiling
salted water for about 15 minutes,
until soft. Drain well and mash with
the sugar, cardamom, and salt and
pepper to taste. Divide into
4 portions and form into balls.

Spread the cornflakes out on a
board. Place the potato balls on the
board and flatten into cakes 7.5-10 cm
(3-4 inches) in diameter. Turn to coat
the other side with cornflakes.

Heat the oil in a frying pan, add
the potato cakes and fry for 3 to
4 minutes on each side until brown,
turning carefully. Transfer to a
warmed serving dish and keep hot.

Pour the cider into the pan, add
the celery, broccoli, and salt and
pepper to taste. Bring to the boil and
boil rapidly for 4 to 5 minutes.

Work the flour into the butter and
add to the pan in small pieces. Bring
to the boil, stirring, until a sauce is
formed. Pour over the patties. Serve
with coleslaw.
Serves 4

Tuna and Oyster Omelet

6 eggs, separated
salt and white pepper
1 tablespoon water
25 g (1 oz) butter
175 g (6 oz) bean
    sprouts
1 × 99 g (3½ oz)
    can tuna fish,
    drained and flaked
1 × 105 g (3.7 oz)
    can smoked
    oysters, drained
SAUCE:
150 g (5.2 oz)
    natural yogurt
1 teaspoon made
    mustard
1 tablespoon lemon
    juice
TO GARNISH:
2 tablespoons
    chopped parsley

Whisk the egg whites with a pinch of salt until soft peaks form. Whisk the yolks with the water and pepper to taste until very frothy. Fold the yolks into the whites.

Melt the butter in a 28 cm (11 inch) omelet pan, turning the pan so the butter coats the base and sides. Add half the bean sprouts, then pour in half the egg mixture and smooth over. Add the remaining bean sprouts, then the remaining egg. Cook for about 5 minutes, lifting the edges occasionally with a palette knife, until firm.

Arrange the tuna around the edge of the omelet, with a ring of oysters inside. Put under a preheated moderate grill for 2 to 3 minutes, until the top is firm and golden.

Meanwhile, mix the sauce ingredients in a small basin.

Scatter the parsley in the centre of the fish. Serve the omelet with the sauce and a tomato and cucumber salad.
Serves 4

Green Bean and Lentil Pie

125 g (4 oz) orange
  lentils
4 celery sticks
1 onion
125 g (4 oz) carrots
1 clove garlic
15 g (½ oz) butter
1 tablespoon oil
227 g (8 oz) frozen
  cut green beans
125 g (4 oz) frozen
  broad beans
1 × 283 g (10 oz)
  can extra thick
  vegetable soup
2 tablespoons
  chopped parsley
2 tablespoons
  chopped mint
125 g (4 oz) smoked
  cheese, grated
salt and pepper
1 × 215 g (7½ oz)
  packet frozen
  shortcrust pastry,
  thawed
milk to glaze
parsley to garnish

Place the lentils in a bowl, cover with boiling water and leave to soak for 1 hour. Drain thoroughly. Slice the celery, onion and carrots. Chop the garlic.

Heat the butter and oil in a flameproof dish, add the celery and sauté until softened; remove. Add the onion and carrots to the dish and sauté until softened. Return the celery to the dish, with the garlic, beans, lentils and soup. Bring to the boil and mix in the parsley, mint, cheese, and salt and pepper to taste. Simmer for 5 minutes.

Roll out the pastry to a circle large enough to cover the dish and decorate with leaves made from the trimmings. Brush with milk and bake in a preheated moderately hot oven, 200°C (400°F), Gas Mark 6, for 40 minutes. Serve hot, garnished with parsley.

Serves 4

Vegetable Medley Casserole

125 g (4 oz) aduki
  beans
125 g (4 oz) mung
  beans
salt and pepper
2 onions, sliced
1 × 397 g (14 oz)
  can chopped
  tomatoes
350 g (12 oz)
  tomatoes, sliced
2 cloves garlic, chopped
3 celery sticks, thinly
  sliced
125 g (4 oz) carrots,
  thinly sliced
2 bouquet garnis
2 tablespoons tomato
  and chilli relish
450 ml (¾ pint)
  vegetable stock
350 g (12 oz) frozen
  cauliflower, thawed
15 g (½ oz) butter,
  melted
2 water biscuits,
  crumbled
50 g (2 oz) Cheddar
  cheese, grated
parsley to garnish

Soak the beans separately in cold water to cover overnight. Drain and rinse. Boil the beans separately in salted water for 10 minutes.

Put the aduki beans in a large flameproof casserole. Cover with half the onions and tomatoes, and the garlic. Place the mung beans on top and cover with the remaining onion, then the celery and carrot, and the remaining chopped tomatoes. Cover with the remaining sliced tomatoes. Tuck the bouquet garnis down the sides. Stir the relish into the stock and pour into the casserole. Bring to the boil, cover and cook in a preheated moderate oven, 180°C (350°F), Gas Mark 4, for 1 hour.

Add salt and pepper to taste and cook, uncovered, for 30 minutes. Discard bouquet garnis.

Toss the cauliflower in the butter. Place on top of the casserole. Mix the biscuits and cheese together and sprinkle over the top.

Increase the oven temperature to 220°C (425°F), Gas Mark 7, and cook for 15 minutes, until golden brown. Garnish with parsley.
Serves 6

Tagliatelle and Sweetcorn

250 g (8 oz) egg
   tagliatelle
salt and pepper
15 g (½ oz) butter
1 tablespoon oil
1 onion, sliced
1 × 326 g (11½ oz)
   can sweetcorn
1 × 35 g (1.25 oz)
   packet sour cream
   sauce mix
120 ml (4 fl oz) milk
1 teaspoon anchovy
   essence
1 teaspoon Worcester-
   shire sauce
TO GARNISH:
chopped parsley
chopped hazelnuts

Cook the tagliatelle in boiling, salted water for 8 minutes. Drain thoroughly and transfer to a warmed serving dish; keep hot.

Melt the butter and oil in the pan, add the onion and sauté for 2 to 3 minutes. Add the drained corn and salt and pepper to taste and heat through.

Make up the sour cream sauce with the milk, as directed on the packet. Add the anchovy essence and Worcestershire sauce.

When the corn mixture is hot, pour over the tagliatelle with three-quarters of the sauce and toss well. Top with the reserved sauce and garnish with parsley and nuts.
Serves 4

Vegetable and Walnut Lasagne

750 g (1½ lb)
   parsnips, diced
salt and pepper
25 g (1 oz) butter
2 tablespoons
   chopped parsley
6 sheets of lasagne
340 g (12 oz)
   cottage cheese
2 × 227 g (8 oz)
   packets frozen
   chopped spinach,
   thawed and drained
¼ teaspoon grated
   nutmeg
50 g (2 oz)
   Emmental cheese,
   thinly sliced
25 g (1 oz) walnuts,
   roughly chopped
1 large tomato, sliced
   and halved
parsley to garnish

Cook the parsnips in boiling salted water in a 1.75 litre (3 pint) shallow flameproof dish for 12 to 15 minutes or until tender. Drain and mash in the dish with half the butter and the parsley.

Cover with half the lasagne, then the cottage cheese, then the remaining lasagne. Cover with the spinach and season with the nutmeg, salt and pepper to taste. Arrange the cheese slices along 2 sides of the dish.

Cook in a preheated moderate oven, 180°C (350°F), Gas Mark 4, for 30 minutes. Sprinkle the walnuts down the centre and dot with the remaining butter. Arrange the tomato slices on either side of the walnuts.

Garnish with parsley and serve hot with crusty bread.
Serves 4

FOREIGN FARE

Alsace Choucroute

1 tablespoon oil
4 thick rashers streaky
  bacon, derinded
4 pork chops,
  trimmed
3 × 283 g (10 oz)
  jars sauerkraut,
  drained
250 g (8 oz) carrots,
  halved lengthways
  then crossways
1 onion, thinly sliced
6 juniper berries,
  lightly crushed
6 black peppercorns
salt
150 ml (¼ pint) dry
  white wine
1 × 283 g (10 oz)
  can potatoes,
  drained
1 × 177 g (6 oz)
  packet frankfurters

Heat the oil in a 2.75 litre (5 pint) flameproof casserole, add the bacon and pork chops and fry until lightly browned. Remove the chops.

Cover the bacon with half the sauerkraut, lay the pork chops on top and cover with the carrots and onion. Spread the remaining sauerkraut over the top and sprinkle with the juniper berries and peppercorns. Season lightly with salt and pour in the wine.

Bring to the boil, cover and cook in a preheated cool oven, 150°C (300°F), Gas Mark 2, for 45 minutes.

Add the potatoes, pushing them down into the sauerkraut. Score the frankfurters in a cross pattern and put on top. Return to the oven and cook for 30 minutes. Serve hot.

Serves 4

New Orleans Jambolaya

2 tablespoons oil
8 chicken thighs
12 mini pork sausages
1 onion, chopped
2 cloves garlic,
  chopped
350 g (12 oz)
  long-grain rice
1 × 539 g (1 lb 3 oz)
  can tomatoes
150 ml (¼ pint) dry
  white wine
1 teaspoon ground
  coriander
¼ teaspoon Tabasco
1 teaspoon salt
pepper
1 green pepper,
  cored, seeded and
  cut into rings
125 g (4 oz) cooked
  prawns in shells,
  tails removed

Heat the oil in a heavy-based pan, add the chicken and sausages and fry until lightly browned; remove. Add the onion and garlic and cook for 1 to 2 minutes. Stir in the rice. Add the tomatoes with their juice, wine, coriander, Tabasco, salt, and pepper to taste. Return the chicken and sausages to the pan. Bring to the boil, cover and simmer for 20 minutes, until the chicken is tender. Remove from the heat and stir.

Place the pepper rings and prawns on top. Cover and leave for about 5 minutes before serving, with a green salad.
Serves 4

Lamb Biriani

1 green chilli
750 g (1½ lb) piece
    fillet half leg of
    lamb
600 ml (1 pint) beef
    stock or water
2 tablespoons
    chopped coriander
5 cm (2 inch) piece
    root ginger, sliced
1 cinnamon stick
1 green pepper,
    cored, seeded and
    quartered
salt and pepper
4 onions
125 g (4 oz) butter
½ teaspoon ground
    cardamom
½ teaspoon ground
    cloves
1 teaspoon ground
    cinnamon
250 g (8 oz)
    basmati rice
75 g (3 oz) seedless
    raisins
½ teaspoon turmeric
2 teaspoons ground
    coriander
2 teaspoons ground
    cumin
8 cloves garlic,
    crushed
50 g (2 oz) blanched
    almonds
25 g (1 oz) shelled
    pistachio nuts
parsley sprig to
    garnish

Cut the chilli lengthways into quarters, taking care to remove seeds.

Put the lamb, stock or water, chopped coriander, ginger, cinnamon stick, chilli and green pepper into a large flameproof casserole. Add salt and pepper to taste. Bring to the boil, cover and simmer for 1½ hours or until the meat is tender. Drain, reserving the stock; make up to 600 ml (1 pint) with water. Cut the meat into bite-sized pieces and set aside.

Cut the onions into quarters, then separate the layers.

Melt the butter, allow to settle, then strain through muslin to clarify. Reheat butter in the pan, add the onions and fry over high heat for 3 to 4 minutes until very lightly browned. Remove with a slotted spoon. Return the meat to the pan with the cardamom, cloves and ground cinnamon and cook, stirring, until the meat is browned. Push to one side of the pan. Add the rice, raisins, turmeric, ground coriander, cumin and garlic and stir-fry for a few minutes.

Add the strained stock and the onions, bring to the boil and simmer for 15 minutes. Adjust the seasoning.

Transfer to a preheated moderate oven, 180°C (350°F), Gas Mark 4, and cook for 10 minutes.

Remove from the oven, discard the cinnamon stick and stir in the nuts. Cover and leave to stand for 5 minutes before serving. Garnish with parsley. Serve with traditional accompaniments.
Serves 4

Boeuf en Daube

15 g (½ oz) butter
1 tablespoon olive oil
1.25 kg (2½ lb)
    topside or top rump,
    rolled and tied
1 teaspoon dry
    mustard
4 onions
4 cloves
175 g (6 oz) smoked
    streaky bacon,
    thickly cut
4 large carrots,
    quartered
8-12 walnut halves
300 ml (½ pint) dry
    red wine
salt
1 parsley sprig
1 thyme sprig
1 bay leaf
7.5 cm (3 inch) piece
    orange rind
6-8 black
    peppercorns

Heat the butter and oil in a deep flameproof casserole. Rub the meat all over with mustard, add to the pan and brown on all sides; remove.

Stud each onion with a clove and brown in the hot fat. Derind the bacon and cut into chunks. Return the beef to the pan and add the bacon, carrots, walnuts, wine, and salt to taste. Tie the herbs and orange rind together and add to the pan with the peppercorns.

Bring to the boil, cover and cook in a preheated cool oven, 140°C (275°F), Gas Mark 1, for 3 hours, turning the meat after 1½ hours. Discard the herbs.

Serve hot or cold with potato salad and crusty French bread.
Serves 6

Greek Lamb with Lettuce

1.5 kg (3-3½ lb) leg
  of lamb
6 cloves garlic,
  halved lengthways
3 tablespoons olive
  oil
3-4 cos lettuces,
  halved lengthways
2 onions, halved
300 ml (½ pint)
  chicken stock
300 ml (½ pint)
  white wine
500 g (1 lb) new
  potatoes
1 × 397 g (14 oz)
  can artichoke
  hearts, drained and
  halved
25 g (1 oz) butter
2 tablespoons plain
  flour
salt and white pepper
3 egg yolks
juice of ½ lemon
parsley to garnish

Make 12 deep incisions in the lamb and push a piece of garlic into each. Heat the oil in a large pan, add the lamb and brown quickly all over.

Place the lettuce and onion around and under the lamb and pour in the stock and wine. Cover and cook slowly for 1½ hours, turning the meat and adding the potatoes and artichokes for the last 20 minutes.

Transfer the lamb and vegetables to a warmed serving dish; keep hot.

Work the butter and flour together and drop, in small pieces, into the liquid remaining in the pan. Bring to the boil, stirring, until thickened and smooth. Remove from the heat and season to taste with salt and pepper.

Whisk the egg yolks and lemon juice together, then stir in a ladleful of the hot liquid from the pan. Add to the pan and cook over a very low heat, stirring, until the liquid thickens a little; do not allow to boil.

Pour a little over the lamb and vegetables and garnish with parsley. Serve the remaining sauce separately.
Serves 6 to 8

Poulet à la Crême

15 g (½ oz) butter
1 tablespoon oil
1.5 kg (3-3½ lb)
    chicken, cut into
    8-10 pieces
3 tablespoons brandy
2 shallots or 1 small
    onion, sliced
3 cloves garlic,
    chopped
1 tablespoon Dijon
    mustard
150 ml (¼ pint) dry
    white wine
1 bunch of mixed
    parsley and
    tarragon
142 ml (5 fl oz)
    single cream
salt and white pepper
250 g (8 oz) button
    mushrooms,
    quartered
2 × 227 g (8 oz)
    packets frozen
    petits pois
3 egg yolks

Heat the butter and oil in a large pan, add the chicken and fry until well browned. Add 2 tablespoons of the brandy and ignite. Remove the chicken.

Add the shallots or onion and garlic to the pan, stir well, then add the mustard, wine, herbs, all but 2 tablespoons of the cream, and salt and pepper to taste. Bring to the boil, replace chicken, cover and simmer for 25 minutes. Add the mushrooms and cook for 10 minutes. Transfer chicken and mushrooms to a serving dish; keep hot.

Add the petits pois to the pan, bring back to the boil and simmer for 4 to 5 minutes. Remove with a slotted spoon and arrange around the chicken. Discard the herbs.

Mix the egg yolks with the remaining cream and brandy. Add 2 tablespoons of the hot sauce and mix well. Pour into the pan and cook very gently, stirring constantly, to make a velvety sauce. Adjust the seasoning and pour over the chicken.
Serves 4

Scandinavian Meatballs

250 g (8 oz) minced
  pork
250 g (8 oz) minced
  veal
grated nutmeg
salt and pepper
50 g (2 oz) butter,
  softened
50 g (2 oz) stale
  white breadcrumbs
2 tablespoons oil
125 g (4 oz) pickled
  sweet-sour
  cucumbers, sliced
  lengthways
1 clove garlic, crushed
50 g (2 oz) egg
  noodles, broken
  into pieces
1 cauliflower, broken
  into florets
300 ml (½ pint)
  chicken stock
142 ml (5 fl oz)
  soured cream
1 teaspoon chopped dill
6-8 pickled baby
  beets, diced
1 tablespoon vinegar

Put the meats in a basin and season
with nutmeg, salt and pepper to
taste. Add the butter and
breadcrumbs and knead together,
adding 1 to 2 teaspoons water if
necessary. Form into about 20 small
balls.

Heat the oil in a large heavy-based
pan, add the meatballs and fry until
lightly browned, shaking the pan
occasionally to prevent them
sticking. Add the cucumber, garlic,
noodles, cauliflower, stock, and
salt and pepper to taste. Bring to
the boil, cover and simmer for
25 minutes.

Transfer to a warmed serving dish.
Pour the soured cream into a circle
on top and sprinkle with the dill.
Toss the beetroot in the vinegar,
drain and pile in the centre. Serve
with crispbreads and cream cheese.
Serves 4

Shanghai Chicken

1 carrot
1 bunch spring onions
50 g (2 oz) egg
 noodles
salt
2 tablespoons oil
5 cm (2 inch) piece
 root ginger, shredded
2-3 cloves garlic,
 sliced
500 g (1 lb) boneless
 chicken breasts,
 very thinly sliced
2 celery sticks, thinly
 sliced
1 × 241 g (8½ oz)
 can bamboo shoots,
 drained and sliced
1 green pepper, cored,
 seeded and shredded
175 g (6 oz) bean
 sprouts
GLAZE:
1 tablespoon
 cornflour
1 tablespoon soy
 sauce
6 tablespoons dry
 sherry
2 tablespoons stock
pinch of chilli powder

Using a sharp knife, make 'V' cuts along the carrot. Cut across into thin slices to form 'flowers'.

Trim the green top and remove the white part from 4 of the spring onions. Carefully shred the tops, leaving 2.5 cm (1 inch) attached at the base. Immerse in iced water until they open out and curl like brushes. Keep on one side for garnish. Finely slice the remaining spring onions.

Put the noodles in a jug and cover with boiling, salted water. Cover and leave for at least 8 minutes.

Mix together the ingredients for the glaze, adding salt to taste.

Heat the oil in a wok or large frying pan. Add the ginger and garlic and stir-fry over high heat for about 1 minute. Add the chicken and stir-fry for a further minute. Add the carrot, onion, celery, bamboo shoots and green pepper and stir-fry for 30 seconds. Drain the noodles, add to the pan with the bean sprouts and stir-fry for 30 seconds.

Add the glaze, turn off the heat and toss until the ingredients are well coated. Garnish with the spring onion brushes and serve at once.
Serves 4

Italian Herby Mussels

25 g (1 oz) butter
2 tablespoons oil
4 celery sticks, sliced
1 red and 1 yellow
  pepper, cored,
  seeded and diced
2 cloves garlic,
  crushed
5 cm (2 inch) strip of
  lemon rind
1 bay leaf
2 litres (3½ pints)
  fresh mussels,
  scrubbed clean
6 tablespoons dry
  white wine
salt and pepper
125 g (4 oz) fresh
  white breadcrumbs
4 eggs
2 tablespoons single
  cream
¼ teaspoon turmeric
2 tablespoons grated
  Parmesan cheese
1 tomato to garnish

Heat the butter and oil in a shallow, flameproof casserole. Add the celery and peppers and sauté until softened.

Add the garlic, lemon rind, bay leaf, mussels (check that none are opened), and wine. Season with salt and pepper to taste.

Cover and cook over high heat for 2 to 3 minutes, shaking the pan constantly. Remove the opened mussels, cover the pan and cook for 1 minute. Discard any mussels which have not opened. Drain and reserve the liquid from the casserole.

Pull off and discard the empty top shell from each mussel. Return the mussels, still in their bottom shells, to the casserole, and sprinkle with the breadcrumbs.

Beat together the eggs, cream, 6 tablespoons of the reserved cooking liquor, turmeric, and salt and pepper to taste. Pour over the mussels and scatter the cheese on top. Cook in a preheated moderately hot oven, 200°C (400°F), Gas Mark 6, for 10 to 15 minutes, until set and golden.

Garnish with tomato quarters and serve with a pasta salad.
Serves 4

Indonesian Meatballs

2 onions
500 g (1 lb) ground
   beef
50 g (2 oz)
   desiccated coconut
2 teaspoons ground
   coriander
2½ tablespoons oil
1 green pepper,
   cored, seeded and
   diced
1 red chilli, seeded
   and sliced
175 g (6 oz)
   long-grain rice
½ teaspoon turmeric
½ teaspoon ground
   ginger
450 ml (¾ pint)
   coconut milk (see
   note) or stock
2 tablespoons
   creamed coconut
   (see note)
TO GARNISH:
1 lime, halved
coriander leaves
   (optional)

Finely chop 1 onion and mix with
the beef, coconut, coriander and
1 teaspoon of the oil; add a little water
to make the mixture cling together.
Form into 32 walnut-sized balls.

Heat the remaining oil in a large
pan, add the meatballs in batches
and fry until browned, shaking the
pan to prevent sticking. Remove
the meatballs and pour off all but
2 tablespoons fat from the pan.

Slice the remaining onion, add to
the pan with the green pepper and
fry until softened. Add the chilli,
rice, turmeric and ginger and stir
well to coat with oil. Add the
coconut milk or stock and the
creamed coconut and stir well.

Bring to the boil and return the
meatballs to the pan. Cover and
simmer for 12 to 15 minutes, until
rice is tender and liquid absorbed.

Pour the juice from one lime half
over the meatballs and rice.

Garnish with remaining lime, cut
into wedges, and coriander, if using.
Serves 4
NOTE: Creamed coconut and coconut
milk are available at delicatessens and
Asian food stores.

SPECIAL OCCASION DISHES

Redcurrant–Glazed Lamb Noisettes

Noisettes are lamb loin, boned, rolled and then cut into thick slices.

125 g (4 oz) button onions
125 g (4 oz) French beans
salt and pepper
15 g (½ oz) butter
1 tablespoon oil
4 × 1.5 cm (¾ inch) thick lamb noisettes
2 tablespoons redcurrant jelly
2 tablespoons lemon juice
2 teaspoons chopped mint
mint sprigs to garnish

Cook the onions and beans in boiling salted water for 8 to 10 minutes; drain and set on one side. Heat the butter and oil in the pan. Season the noisettes with salt and pepper, add to the pan and fry over high heat for 3 minutes each side; remove.

Heat the redcurrant jelly and lemon juice in the pan, stirring until the jelly dissolves to form a glaze. Return the meat, turning until coated, then add the vegetables and reheat.

Transfer to a warmed serving dish, sprinkle with the chopped mint and garnish with mint sprigs. Serve with crusty rolls and a green salad.

Serves 2

Veal with Tuna Cream Sauce

2 veal escalopes
salt and pepper
15 g (½ oz) butter
1 tablespoon oil
125 g (4 oz) courgettes
1 onion, sliced
125 g (4 oz) baby
  carrots
300 ml (½ pint)
  chicken stock
1 × 99 g (3½ oz)
  can tuna, drained
142 ml (5 fl oz)
  soured cream
2 teaspoons cornflour
TO GARNISH:
8 green olives, sliced
4 lemon slices

Beat the meat until very thin and season with salt and pepper. Heat the butter and oil in a pan and sauté the veal until browned on each side; remove from pan.

Cut the courgettes into quarters lengthwise. Add to pan with the onion, carrots and stock. Cover and simmer for 10 to 12 minutes or until the carrots are tender.

Flake the tuna and mash with the cream. Add cornflour and blend until smooth, then add to the pan and bring to the boil. Replace veal and simmer for 3 minutes until hot.

Garnish with olives and lemon.
Serves 2

Carpetbag Steak

750 g (1½ lb) rump
    steak in one piece,
    5 cm (2 inches)
    thick
salt and pepper
cayenne pepper
1 × 250 g (8 oz)
    can oysters
25 g (1 oz) butter
1 tablespoon oil
250 g (8 oz)
    potatoes, boiled
    and sliced
2 large tomatoes,
    quartered
chopped chives
1-2 tablespoons
    white wine
    (optional)

Cut a pocket in the steak lengthways.
Season the steak inside and out, with
salt, pepper and cayenne to taste. Put
the oysters in the pocket, reserving
the liquid. Sew up the opening or
secure with long cocktail sticks.

Melt half the butter and the oil in
a heavy-based pan over a high
heat, add the steak and brown for
4 minutes on each side. Lower the
heat and cook for 20 minutes,
turning twice. Add the potatoes
and tomatoes to the pan for the
last 10 minutes.

Transfer to a warmed serving dish.
Sprinkle the potatoes and tomatoes
with chopped chives.

Add 3 tablespoons of the oyster
liquid, making up with white wine if
necessary, and the remaining butter
to the pan and bring to the boil,
stirring well to scrape the sediment
from the pan.

To serve, cut the steak into slices
and pour over the sauce. Serve with
a green salad.

Serves 4

Rosy Duckling

1 onion, studded
 with 2 cloves
small bunch of
 parsley
1 × 2 kg (4½ lb)
 duckling, wiped
 and dried
salt and pepper
1 × 411 g (14½ oz)
 can pear halves
2 red peppers, cored,
 seeded and cut into
 strips
1 tablespoon white
 peppercorns
50 g (2 oz) fresh or
 frozen and thawed
 raspberries
1 teaspoon arrowroot,
 blended with
 2 tablespoons cold
 water
watercress to garnish

Put the onion and parsley inside the duckling and season well, inside and out, with salt and pepper.

Place on a rack in a roasting pan and cook in a preheated moderately hot oven, 200°C (400°F), Gas Mark 6, for 45 minutes. Pour off all the fat and place the duckling in the pan. Add the pears, with their syrup, peppers and peppercorns. Cook for a further 45 minutes, basting frequently; cover the breast with foil if it browns too quickly.

Transfer to a warmed serving dish. Fill each pear half with 3 or 4 raspberries and arrange at one end of the bird, the pepper strips at the other.

Skim off the fat from the liquid in the pan. Add remaining raspberries and bring to the boil. Boil to reduce a little, then mash the raspberries into the liquid. Strain and return to the pan. Add the blended arrowroot and cook, stirring, until thickened.

Garnish the duckling with watercress; serve with the sauce.
Serves 4

Salmon Steaks with Herb Butter Sauce

250 g (8 oz) carrots,
    cut into fine
    julienne strips
salt and pepper
75 g (3 oz) unsalted
    butter
1 tablespoon oil
6 × 175 g (6 oz)
    salmon steaks
350 g (12 oz)
    cucumber, peeled
150 ml (¼ pint) dry
    white wine
2 tablespoons
    chopped tarragon
2 tablespoons
    chopped chervil
1 tablespoon chopped
    chives

Cook the carrots in boiling salted water in a large pan for 1 minute; drain and leave on one side.

Melt 25 g (1 oz) of the butter and the oil in the same pan. Sprinkle the salmon steaks with salt and pepper to taste, add to the pan and fry for 5 to 7 minutes on each side. Transfer to a warmed serving dish and keep hot.

Cut the cucumber in half lengthways, remove the seeds and cut into 1 cm (½ inch) slices. Add to the pan with the carrots and wine, cover and cook for 4 to 5 minutes. Remove with a slotted spoon and arrange around the fish; keep warm. Boil the liquor in the pan until it is reduced to 2 tablespoons.

Beat together the tarragon, chervil, chives and remaining butter in a basin. Beat in the reduced liquor until a smooth, thick herb sauce is obtained. Spoon onto the salmon and serve with wholewheat rolls.

Serves 6

Braised Beef in Guinness

1.25 kg (2½ lb)
  chuck steak
25 g (1 oz) butter
2 tablespoons oil
3 onions, chopped
1 tablespoon brandy
600 ml (1 pint)
  Guinness
1 bouquet garni
500 g (1 lb) young
  carrots
250 g (8 oz) baby
  turnips, halved
500 g (1 lb)
  aubergines, cut
  into bite-sized
  pieces
salt and pepper
6 mushrooms
TO GARNISH:
3 tablespoons
  chopped basil and
  1 basil sprig
finely shredded rind
  of ½ lemon
6 black olives

Cut the steak into 5 × 7.5 cm
(2 × 3 inch) pieces. Heat the butter
and oil in a large flameproof
casserole or pan, add the beef and fry
until well browned.

Add the onions and cook until
beginning to soften. Add the brandy
and ignite. Add the Guinness,
bouquet garni, carrots, turnips,
aubergine, and salt and pepper to
taste.

Bring to the boil and cook very
gently for about 3 hours, until the
meat is very tender. Add the
mushrooms for the last 30 minutes.
Discard the bouquet garni.

Mix the chopped basil and lemon
rind together and sprinkle over the
top. Scatter over the olives and
garnish with the basil sprig.

Serve with crusty bread and a
spinach salad.
Serves 6

Fondue Gîtane

1 × 1.25 kg (2½ lb)
  chicken, with
  giblets
600 ml (1 pint) water
600 ml (1 pint) dry
  white wine
1 onion, chopped
1 bay leaf and
  parsley sprig, tied
  together
salt and pepper
250 g (8 oz) fillet
  steak
250 g (8 oz) pork
  fillet
4 lambs' kidneys
175 g (6 oz) button
  onions
175 g (6 oz) new
  potatoes
TO SERVE:
sauce tartare
tomato and chilli
  sauce
curried mayonnaise
peach chutney
Dijon mustard

Put the chicken in a deep, flameproof casserole. Add the water, wine, chicken giblets, onion, herbs, and salt and pepper to taste. Bring to the boil, cover and simmer for 45 minutes or until the chicken is tender. Discard giblets. Cut chicken flesh into large pieces.

Cut the steak and pork into finger-sized strips. Halve and core the kidneys, then cut in half again.

Add the onions and potatoes to the stock and bring back to the boil. Place on the table, over a source of heat to keep it simmering.

Arrange the meats on 8 plates. Place the accompaniments in bowls.

To eat, thread a piece of chicken or meat onto a long-handled fork and plunge into the stock until hot, if chicken, or cooked to taste. Dip into sauces on your plate to eat.

When the meat is finished, discard the herbs from the casserole and divide the onions, potatoes and cooking stock between 8 soup bowls.
Serves 8

Guinea Fowl with Grapes

50 g (2 oz) butter
2 tablespoons oil
2 guinea fowl, each
  cut into 4 pieces
8 shallots
500 g (1 lb) seedless
  black grapes
450 ml (¾ pint) grape
  juice (unsweetened)
300 ml (½ pint) dry
  white wine
salt and pepper
350 g (12 oz) brown
  rice
3 tablespoons
  chopped tarragon

Heat half the butter and the oil in a large flameproof casserole. Sauté the guinea fowl until well browned.

Add the shallots, 350 g (12 oz) of the grapes, the grape juice, wine, and salt and pepper to taste.

Cover and cook in a preheated moderate oven, 160°C (325°F), Gas Mark 3, for 20 minutes.

Stir in the rice and cook for 35 to 40 minutes or until the birds are tender and the rice is cooked. Stir in the remaining butter and tarragon.

Garnish with the remaining grapes and serve with a watercress salad.
Serves 8

Roast Leg of Lamb Parma

227 g (8 oz) frozen
  chopped spinach,
  thawed
ground mace
salt and pepper
5 slices Parma or
  other smoked ham,
  halved crossways
2.25-2.5 kg (5-5¾ lb)
  leg of lamb
2 tablespoons oil
10 small potatoes
5 onions, halved
450 ml (¾ pint) dry
  white wine
1 × 397 g (14 oz)
  can artichokes,
  drained
chopped parsley to
  garnish

Squeeze the spinach until dry, then mix in mace, salt and pepper to taste. Put a portion on each piece of ham and roll into small cylinders.

Make 10 deep slashes at regular intervals in the lamb and insert the ham. Sprinkle with salt and pepper.

Heat the oil in a roasting pan, add the meat and baste. Cook in a pre-heated moderately hot oven, 200°C (400°F), Gas Mark 6, allowing 20 minutes per 500 g (1 lb) plus 15 minutes. Add the potatoes and onions to the pan for the last hour; season and baste well.

Transfer the lamb and vegetables to a large dish. Keep hot.

Drain off the fat from the pan, pour in the wine and heat gently, stirring to incorporate the sediment in the pan. Add the artichokes and heat through for about 3 minutes, then add to the lamb. Sprinkle the potatoes with parsley; serve the sauce separately.
Serves 10

Bouillabaisse with Rouille

1.2 litres (2 pints)
   wine and water,
   mixed
2 fennel bulbs,
   quartered
2 bay leaves
2 leeks, chopped
pared rind of
   ½ orange
few thyme sprigs
3 onions, chopped
¼ teaspoon
   powdered saffron
4 tablespoons olive
   oil
1 red pepper, halved,
   cored and seeded
salt and pepper
1.75 g (4 lb) fish, cut
   into 5 cm (2 inch)
   chunks (see note)
1 small cooked crab
pinch of chilli powder
150 ml (¼ pint)
   mayonnaise

Put all the ingredients, except the
fish, chilli powder and mayonnaise,
in a large pan, adding salt and pepper
to taste. Bring to the boil and boil
rapidly for 5 minutes. Take out the
red pepper and add all the fish. Boil
rapidly for about 12 to 14 minutes,
until the fish is tender but not
broken. Discard the bay leaves,
orange rind and thyme.

Meanwhile, pound the red pepper
with a pinch each of salt and chilli
powder until smooth. Fold into the
mayonnaise to make the rouille.

Serve the bouillabaisse in
individual bowls, dividing the crab
between each. Accompany with
French bread, dried in the oven, and
top with rouille.

Serves 10

NOTE: Choose from halibut, turbot,
eel, grey mullet, bass, hake, cod,
haddock or whiting.

SLOW COOKER MEALS

Slow cookers cook food very gently over a long period. They can be turned on and left to cook food overnight or whilst out at work or at leisure. Food which is cooked completely in a slow cooker cannot be browned first, so special attention must be paid to colour and presentation.

The order of adding food to the pot – vegetables first, then meat – is important. Avoid using large chunks of vegetables as manufacturers agree they tend to cook more slowly than meat at the low temperatures used. Some manufacturers recommend that all dried beans and pulses should first be boiled for 10 minutes before cooking in a slow cooker.

Green-leafed vegetables cannot be cooked successfully in a slow cooker as they need to be cooked quickly over a high heat if they are to be appetizing. It's a good idea, therefore, to serve green vegetables separately as a crunchy salad to contrast with the softer-textured dishes.

Chicken and Leek Soup

750 g (1½ lb) leeks,
  white part only,
  thinly sliced
1 bay leaf
2 potatoes, diced
25 g (1 oz) pearl
  barley
2 small onions, each
  cut into 8 pieces
few parsley stalks
175 g (6 oz) stewing
  steak, in 2 pieces
500 g (1 lb) chicken
  pieces, or ½ chicken
125 g (4 oz) chicken
  giblets
600 ml (1 pint) water
salt and pepper
175 g (6 oz) ready-to-
  eat jumbo prunes
chopped parsley to
  garnish

Put all the ingredients, except the prunes, in the stoneware pot, seasoning with salt and pepper to taste.

Cook on *High* for 4 hours, adding the prunes for the last 30 minutes, or on *Low* for 8 hours, adding the prunes for the last hour.

Cut the beef and chicken into pieces and return to the soup. Discard the bay leaf and giblets. Garnish with parsley and serve with hot crusty bread.

Serves 4

Spiced Silverside

1 large onion,
    quartered
500 g (1 lb) carrots,
    sliced
500 g (1 lb) small
    potatoes
salt and pepper
1 kg (2 lb) spiced,
    cured silverside
1 bouquet garni
½ pint boiling water
DUMPLINGS:
125 g (4 oz)
    self-raising flour
pinch of salt
50 g (2 oz) shredded
    suet
1 tablespoon chopped
    parsley
¼ teaspoon ground
    bay leaves
3-4 tablespoons
    water
TO GARNISH:
chopped parsley

Place the onion, carrots and potatoes in the stoneware pot and sprinkle very lightly with salt and pepper. Put the meat in the centre and press into the vegetables. Add the bouquet garni and boiling water.

Cook on *High* for 5 hours, or on *High* for 1 hour, then *Low* for 8 to 9 hours.

To make the dumplings, sift the flour and salt into a bowl. Stir in the suet, herbs and enough water to make a soft dough. Knead lightly, then divide into 8 and roll into balls. Drop the dumplings into the pot and cook on *High* for a further 30 minutes.

Slice the meat thinly and arrange on a warmed serving dish, with the vegetables and dumplings down either side. Garnish with parsley. Discard the bouquet garni and serve the cooking liquid as a sauce.

Serves 4 to 6

Rabbit with Mustard Sauce

2 large carrots
1 large onion,
   coarsely chopped
salt and pepper
125 g (4 oz) streaky
   bacon, derinded
   and cut into strips
1 bay leaf
a little grated lemon
   rind
750 g (1½ lb)
   boneless rabbit
1 tablespoon dry
   mustard
150 ml (¼ pint) dry
   cider
1 × 213 g (7½ oz)
   can button mush-
   rooms, drained
2 tablespoons Dijon
   mustard
3 tablespoons soured
   cream
lemon balm sprig to
   garnish

Cut the carrots into long, thin strips with a potato peeler. Place in the stoneware pot with the onion and sprinkle with salt and pepper. Add the bacon, bay leaf and lemon rind. Coat the rabbit with the dry mustard and sprinkle with salt and pepper to taste. Arrange on top and pour in the cider.

Cook on *High* for 3½ hours. After 3¼ hours, drain off and reserve the liquid from the pot. Add the mushrooms to the pot. Quickly mix together the mustard and cream. Add 6 tablespoons of the cooking liquid and stir well. Pour into the pot and complete the cooking. Discard bay leaf.

Alternatively, cook on *Low* for 7 hours, adding the mushrooms, mustard and cream as above after 6½ hours.

Garnish with lemon balm and serve with a green salad.
Serves 4

Lamb with Lentils

350 g (12 oz)
  carrots, sliced
125 g (4 oz)
  parsnips, sliced
1 clove garlic,
  crushed
1 bay leaf
125 g (4 oz) orange
  lentils, soaked for
  1 hour
salt and pepper
150 ml (¼ pint) red
  wine
750 g (1½ lb) lamb
  brochettes or lamb
  leg fillet, cubed
2 tablespoons soy
  sauce
175 g (6 oz) button
  mushrooms
parsley sprigs to
  garnish

Place the carrots, parsnips, garlic,
bay leaf and drained lentils in the
stoneware pot and season with salt
and pepper to taste. Pour in the
wine.

Brush the meat all over with the
soy sauce and sprinkle with salt and
pepper. Place on top of the
vegetables.

Cook on *High* for 4 hours, adding
the mushrooms for the last
30 minutes, or on *Low* for 8 hours,
adding the mushrooms for the last
hour.

Discard the bay leaf. Garnish with
parsley and serve with a crisp green
salad.

Serves 4

Pork and Peach Casserole

750 g (1½ lb) pork
   shoulder steaks
juice of ½ lemon
1 tablespoon oil
1 teaspoon dried basil
10 white peppercorns,
   crushed
500 g (1 lb) button
   onions, or small
   onions, halved
4 celery sticks, sliced
salt
1 × 411 g (14½ oz)
   can peach halves
227 g (8 oz) frozen
   broad beans,
   partially thawed
2 teaspoons
   Worcestershire
   sauce
basil to garnish

Place the pork steaks in a dish. Pour over the lemon juice and oil, add the basil and peppercorns and leave to marinate for at least 1 hour.

Place the onions and celery in the stoneware pot, with salt to taste. Arrange the pork on top and place a peach half on each. Pour in the peach syrup. Cook on *High* for 4 hours, adding the beans for the last hour.

Arrange the pork on a warmed dish. Slice 1 peach half and put a piece on each steak. Arrange the vegetables around them; keep hot.

Skim the fat from the liquid left in the pot. Place half the cooking liquid, the remaining peaches, and the Worcestershire sauce in a blender and blend to make a sauce. Pour over the meat and garnish with basil.

Serves 4

Caraway Veal

500 g (1 lb) carrots,
   sliced diagonally
1 large onion, sliced
4 veal shoulder slices
salt and pepper
4 slices cooked ham
4 × 2.5 cm (1 inch)
   strips lemon rind
½ teaspoon chilli
   powder
2 tablespoons tomato
   purée
1 chicken stock cube
1 teaspoon caraway
   seeds
227 g (8 oz) frozen
   sliced green beans,
   partially thawed
1 × 425 g (15 oz) can
   cannellini beans
4 tablespoons soured
   cream

Place the carrots and onion in the stoneware pot. Sprinkle each veal slice with salt and pepper and wrap in a slice of ham. Place on top of the vegetables, add a strip of lemon rind to each and sprinkle with the chilli powder.

Combine the tomato purée, stock cube and caraway seeds in a jug and make up to 150 ml (¼ pint) with boiling water. Pour into the pot.

Cook on *High* for 5 hours, adding the green beans and drained cannellini beans for the last hour, or on *Low* for 10 hours, adding the beans for the last 1½ hours.

Transfer the meat to a warmed serving dish and surround with the vegetables and liquid. Trickle a little soured cream over the meat.

Serves 4

Stuffed Mackerel with Gooseberry Sauce

1 onion, sliced
4 small mackerel, cleaned
salt and pepper
1 × 283 g (10 oz) can gooseberries
15 g (½ oz) fresh white breadcrumbs
pinch of ground allspice
5 cm (2 inch) strip orange rind, shredded
few tarragon leaves, chopped
4 tablespoons tarragon vinegar
1 × 539 g (19 oz) can new potatoes, drained

SAUCE:
1 tablespoon horseradish sauce
2 tablespoons soured cream

Place half the onion in the stoneware pot. Sprinkle the inside of the mackerel with salt. Drain the gooseberries, reserving the syrup, and chop half of them. Mix with the breadcrumbs, allspice, orange rind, chopped tarragon, and pepper to taste; use to stuff the mackerel. Place in the stoneware pot and cover with the remaining onion. Pour in the vinegar and 4 tablespoons of the gooseberry syrup.

Cook on *High* for 2 hours, adding the potatoes for the last 30 minutes, or on *Low* for 4 hours, adding the potatoes for the last hour.

Work the remaining gooseberries and syrup in a blender to make a purée. Mix with the horseradish, cream, and salt and pepper to taste to make the sauce.

Serve the mackerel hot with a mixed salad. Serve the sauce separately.
Serves 4

Ham and Pea Chowder

2 onions, sliced
2 celery sticks, sliced
1 large potato, sliced
2 bay leaves
125 g (4 oz) split
  peas, soaked for
  3-4 hours
2 small bacon hocks,
  soaked for 1 hour
300 ml (½ pint)
  water
1 × 539 g (19 oz)
  can new potatoes,
  drained
227 g (8 oz) frozen
  broad beans,
  partially thawed
salt and pepper
1-2 tablespoons milk
  (optional)
TO GARNISH:
2 hard-boiled eggs,
  chopped (optional)
2 tablespoons
  chopped mint
1 mint sprig

Place the onions, celery, sliced potato, bay leaves and drained peas in the stoneware pot. Place the drained hocks on top and add the water.

Cook on *High* for 5 hours, adding the canned potatoes and broad beans for the last 30 minutes, or on *Low* for 10 to 11 hours, adding the potatoes and beans for the last hour. Check the seasoning and, if necessary, add salt and pepper.

Transfer the canned potatoes and broad beans to a warmed soup tureen with a slotted spoon. Cut the meat from the hocks into small pieces, discarding the skin and bones, and add to the tureen.

Work the remaining contents of the pot in a blender or food processor to make a purée, adding a little milk if too thick. Pour over the meat and vegetables. Garnish with the eggs, if using, and mint.
Serves 4

Braised Lambs' Hearts

500 g (1 lb) onions,
  sliced
1 teaspoon dried sage
salt and pepper
250 g (8 oz) carrots,
  sliced diagonally
3 celery sticks, sliced
4 lambs' hearts
2 teaspoons yeast
  extract
150 ml (¼ pint)
  boiling water
75 g (3 oz)
  wholewheat bread,
  diced
TO GARNISH:
4 tablespoons natural
  yogurt
1 small green pepper,
  cored, seeded and
  cut into rings

Put the onions in the stoneware pot and sprinkle with the sage, and salt and pepper to taste. Add the carrots and celery and season with salt and pepper to taste.

Wash the hearts well, trim, removing any blood vessels, and season with salt and pepper, inside and out. Place on top of the vegetables, pressing them down a little. Dissolve the yeast extract in the boiling water and pour into the pot.

Cook on *High* for 5 hours, adding the bread for the last 30 minutes, or on *Low* for 10 hours, adding the bread for the last hour.

Slice the hearts thickly and arrange on a warmed serving dish; keep hot. Work the contents of the pot in a blender or food processor to make a sauce and serve with the hearts. Trickle the yogurt over the hearts and arrange the pepper on top.

Serve with a crisp green salad.

Serves 4

Liver Provençal

2 teaspoons oil
3 cloves garlic
3 celery sticks, sliced
1 leek, white part
  only, thinly sliced
6 thin slices Parma
  or other smoked
  ham, halved
500 g (1 lb) lambs'
  liver, cut into
  12 thin slices
pinch of ground bay
  leaves
pepper
12 cloves
150 ml (¼ pint) red
  wine
1 × 439 g (15½ oz)
  can red kidney
  beans, drained and
  rinsed
1 × 397 g (14 oz)
  can young carrots,
  drained
chopped chives to
  garnish

Spread the oil on the base of the stoneware pot. Crush 2 cloves garlic and spear the other one on a wooden cocktail stick. Add to the pot with the celery and half the leek.

Place each halved ham slice on a board and lay a piece of liver on top. Sprinkle with ground bay leaves and pepper. Fold two sides of ham into the centre, overlapping, and secure with a clove. Place on top of the vegetables and sprinkle with the remaining leek. Pour in the wine.

Cook on *High* for 2½ hours, adding the beans and carrots for the last 30 minutes, or on *Low* for 5 hours, adding the beans and carrots for the last hour. Remove the speared garlic.

Garnish with chives and serve with a green salad.
Serves 4

Main Meal Minestrone

2 cloves garlic
4 celery sticks
250 g (8 oz) cabbage
50 g (2 oz) spaghetti
350 g (12 oz) streaky
　bacon, derinded
4 carrots, sliced
2 onions, chopped
2 potatoes, diced
2 courgettes, sliced
25 g (1 oz) Italian
　rice
125 g (4 oz) mange-
　tout or frozen green
　beans, thawed
1 bouquet garni
350 g (12 oz) Italian
　mortadella, thickly
　sliced
1 × 411 g (14½ oz)
　can haricot beans,
　drained
1 × 397 g (14 oz)
　can tomatoes
150 ml (¼ pint)
　chicken stock
salt and pepper

Crush the garlic and slice the celery and cabbage. Break the spaghetti into short lengths and dice the bacon.

Place all the ingredients, except the cabbage, in the stoneware pot, seasoning with salt and pepper to taste.

Cook on *High* for 3 hours, adding the cabbage for the last 30 minutes, or on *Low* for 6 hours, adding the cabbage for the last hour. Stir when the cabbage is added and, if necessary, add a little more stock. Discard the bouquet garni.

Serve with bread rolls and grated Parmesan cheese.
Serves 4

Vegetables in Cider Sauce

1 clove garlic, cut
1 teaspoon olive oil
175 g (6 oz) young
    turnips, sliced
1 Spanish onion
salt and pepper
350 g (12 oz) carrots
1 fennel bulb
125 g (4 oz) potato
2 tomatoes, sliced
1 teaspoon dill seeds
2 teaspoons mustard
    seeds
1 teaspoon dried
    oregano
1 bouquet garni
150 ml (¼ pint) dry
    cider
1 × 397 g (14 oz)
    can borlotti beans
TO GARNISH:
150 g (5.2 oz)
    natural yogurt
2 tablespoons pine
    nuts

Rub the stoneware pot with the cut
surface of the garlic and spread the
olive oil over the base. Place turnip
in the pot. Finely chop the onion and
sprinkle some in the pot with salt
and pepper to taste. Thinly slice the
carrots and fennel, and dice the
potato. Arrange in layers in the pot
with the tomato, sprinkling each
layer with onion and salt and pepper.
Sprinkle the dill, mustard seeds and
oregano over the top and add the
bouquet garni. Pour in the cider.

Cook on *High* for 3½ hours,
adding the beans for the last
30 minutes, or on *Low* for 7 hours,
adding the beans for the last hour.
Discard the bouquet garni.

Transfer to a warmed serving dish,
pour the yogurt in a circle on top and
sprinkle with the nuts.

Serve with garlic bread.

Serves 4

PRESSURE COOKER MEALS

Pressure cookers save time and fuel and although they excel at tenderizing tough meat cuts, they can also cook delicate vegetables, fish and pulses to perfection, preserving and boosting natural flavours. Neither colour, texture nor shape are impaired if timing and instructions are correctly followed, and food cut in the suggested sizes.

The steam which escapes from a conventional saucepan is retained in a pressure cooker, increasing the temperature at which liquids boil and thus speeding up the cooking process. Timing is vitally important – with some foods a matter of only a minute or two of extra cooking can ruin their texture and flavour. So follow these recipes and the instructions supplied with your particular cooker carefully.

Boiled Salt Beef with Dates and Figs

1.25 kg (2½ lb)
  cured salt beef
1 teaspoon dry
  mustard
250 g (8 oz)
  courgettes
2 tablespoons oil
1 onion, sliced
300 ml (½ pint)
  white wine, cider
  or stock
1 cinnamon stick
1 cauliflower, broken
  into florets
1 large carrot, sliced
250-500 g (8 oz-1 lb)
  potatoes (optional)
175 g (6 oz) figs,
  fresh or dried
50 g (2 oz) stoned
  dates
2 tablespoons plain
  flour, blended with
  2 tablespoons water

Rub the beef all over with mustard. Leave to stand for 15 minutes.

Cut the courgettes in half, then slice lengthways.

Heat the oil in the pressure cooker, add the onion and sauté for about 3 minutes. Add the beef and brown on all sides. Add the wine, cider or stock and cinnamon.

Seal the cooker and bring to *High* pressure. Cook for 35 minutes. Reduce the pressure quickly.

Add the vegetables and fruits, seal and bring back to *High* pressure. Cook for 4 minutes. Reduce the pressure quickly. Transfer the meat, vegetables and fruit to a warmed serving dish. Discard the cinnamon.

Pour the blended flour into the cooker and bring to the boil, stirring. Boil for 3 minutes, until thickened. Serve the sauce with the meat, cut into slices.
Serves 6

Chick Pea and Bacon Stew

250 g (8 oz) boiling
  bacon
250 g (8 oz) bratwurst
250 g (8 oz) cabanos
125 g (4 oz) chick
  peas, soaked
  overnight
350 g (12 oz) carrots
2 tablespoons oil
4 onions, quartered
300 ml (½ pint)
  chicken stock
¼-½ teaspoon chilli
  powder
½ teaspoon paprika
2 small heads spring
  greens, quartered
salt and pepper
chopped parsley

Cut the bacon into 4 chunks. Cut the bratwurst into thick chunks. Cut the cabanos into 7.5 cm (3 inch) pieces. Drain and rinse the chick peas. Slice the carrots thickly.

Heat the oil in the pressure cooker, add the onions and carrots and fry until softened. Add the meats, chick peas, stock, chilli powder and paprika.

Seal the cooker and bring to *High* pressure. Cook for 25 minutes. Reduce the pressure quickly. Add the greens, seal and bring back to *High* pressure for 4 minutes. Reduce the pressure quickly.

Check the seasoning, garnish with parsley and serve with rye bread.
Serves 4

Haricot Lamb

250 g (8 oz) haricot
  beans, soaked
  overnight
1 tablespoon oil
4 lamb chump or
  shoulder chops
1 large onion, sliced
450 ml (¾ pint)
  chicken stock
1 bouquet garni
500 g (1 lb) carrots,
  quartered
350 g (12 oz) leeks,
  cut into 5 cm
  (2 inch) lengths
1 tablespoon tomato
  purée
salt and pepper
1 tablespoon cornflour,
  blended with
  2 tablespoons water
1 tablespoon capers

Drain and rinse the beans.

Heat the oil in the cooker, add the chops and brown on both sides. Add the onion, stock, beans and bouquet garni. Bring to the boil, uncovered, then lower the heat until the contents are boiling gently.

Seal and bring to *High* pressure on the same heat. Cook for 15 minutes. Reduce the pressure slowly.

Add the carrots, leeks, tomato purée, and salt and pepper to taste. Follow the procedure above and cook for 4 minutes. Reduce the pressure slowly.

Strain the contents of the pan. Arrange the meat and vegetables on a warmed serving dish. Return the liquid to the cooker. Add the blended cornflour and the capers. Bring to the boil, stirring, until thickened. Pour over the meat and vegetables. Serve with crusty bread.
Serves 4

Mediterranean-Style Tripe

750 g-1 kg (1½-2 lb)
    ox tripe
2 tablespoons olive
    oil
2 onions, sliced
3 large cloves garlic,
    chopped
4 tablespoons tomato
    purée
¾ teaspoon salt
1 teaspoon sugar
¼ teaspoon chilli
    powder
pepper
1 red and 1 green
    pepper, cored,
    seeded and
    quartered
125 g (4 oz) carrot,
    cut lengthways
    into large strips
75 g (3 oz) quick-
    cook macaroni
1 × 397 g (14 oz)
    can artichoke
    hearts
2 tablespoons
    chopped marjoram
marjoram sprig to
    garnish

Cut the tripe into 7.5 cm (3 inch)
pieces.

Heat the oil in the pressure cooker,
add the onions and garlic and fry
until softened. Add the tripe and
cook for 2 to 3 minutes. Mix
together the tomato purée, salt,
sugar, chilli powder and pepper to
taste in a jug and make up to 300 ml
(½ pint) with water; add to the
pressure cooker.

Seal the cooker and bring to *High*
pressure. Cook for 10 minutes.
Reduce the pressure quickly.

Add the peppers, carrot and
macaroni, making sure all macaroni
is below the level of the liquid. Seal
and bring back to *High* pressure.
Cook for 10 minutes. Reduce the
pressure quickly.

Drain and halve the artichokes and
add to the cooker. Stir in the
marjoram. Heat through gently in
the open pan for 3 to 5 minutes.

Garnish with marjoram to serve.
Serves 4

Fruity Pigeons in Cider

4 wood pigeons
salt and pepper
175 g (6 oz)
   pre-soaked apricots
50 g (2 oz) sultanas
4 thyme sprigs
8 rashers streaky
   bacon, derinded
25 g (1 oz) butter
1 tablespoon oil
1 large onion,
   chopped
1 bay leaf
2 apples, peeled,
   quartered and
   cored
150 ml (¼ pint)
   sweet vermouth
1 spring cabbage,
   quartered
1 × 439 g (15½ oz)
   can chestnuts,
   drained
1 tablespoon plain
   flour

Season the pigeons inside and out with salt and pepper. Use half the apricots and the sultanas to stuff the pigeons, adding a thyme sprig to each. Wrap each pigeon in 2 bacon rashers, securing with a cocktail stick.

Heat half the butter and the oil in the pressure cooker, add the pigeons and brown well all over. Leave them breast side down and add the remaining apricots, the onion, bay leaf, apples and vermouth.

Seal the cooker and bring to *High* pressure. Cook for 40 minutes. Reduce the pressure quickly. Add the cabbage, chestnuts and a little salt. Seal and bring back to *High* pressure. Cook for 4 minutes. Reduce the pressure quickly. Transfer the pigeons to a warmed serving dish.

Strain the contents of the pan and arrange the fruit, cabbage and chestnuts with the pigeons; keep warm.

Return the liquid to the cooker. Work the remaining butter and the flour together and add to the cooker in small pieces. Cook, stirring, until thickened. Serve with the pigeons.
Serves 4

Veal Blanquette

750 g (1½ lb) veal
  shoulder, cubed
500 g (1 lb) large
  carrots, halved
2 onions, quartered
2 celery sticks, cut in
  quarters
300 ml (½ pint)
  white wine
1 bouquet garni
salt and white pepper
15 g (½ oz) butter
1 tablespoon plain
  flour
1 egg yolk
3 tablespoons single
  cream
parsley to garnish

Place the veal, vegetables, wine,
bouquet garni, and salt and pepper to
taste in the cooker. Seal and bring to
High pressure. Cook for 15 minutes.
Reduce the pressure quickly. Discard
the bouquet garni.

Work the butter and flour together
and add to the cooker in small pieces.
Cook uncovered for a few minutes,
stirring, until thickened. Remove
from heat. Mix the egg yolk with the
cream, add a little of the hot stock,
then add to the cooker and stir until
blended.

Pour into a warmed serving dish,
garnish with parsley and serve with
French bread.
Serves 4

Oxtail with Grapes

25 g (1 oz) dripping
  or lard
1.25 kg (2½ lb)
  oxtail, jointed and
  trimmed
1 large onion,
  chopped
500 g (1 lb) large
  carrots, halved
  lengthways
300 ml (½ pint)
  boiling beef stock
300 ml (½ pint)
  white wine
250 g (½ lb) seedless
  green grapes
salt and pepper
175 g (6 oz)
  quick-cook
  macaroni
grapes to garnish
  (optional)

Melt the fat in the pressure cooker,
add the meat in two batches and fry
until well browned; remove. Add the
onion and fry for 1 to 2 minutes, then
add the carrots, stock, meat, wine,
grapes, and salt and pepper to taste.

Seal the cooker and bring to *High*
pressure. Cook for 40 minutes.
Reduce the pressure quickly.

Strain, reserving the liquid and the
ingredients separately. Pour all but
120 ml (4 fl oz) of the liquor back
into the cooker and add the
macaroni. Seal and bring back to
High pressure. Cook for 6 minutes.
Reduce the pressure quickly.

Meanwhile, arrange the oxtail on a
large, warmed serving dish with the
carrots down one side; keep hot.

Place the reserved onion, grapes
and stock in a blender or food
processor and work to a sauce.

Arrange the macaroni on the other
side of the meat. Pour over the sauce
and garnish with grapes, if wished.
Serves 4

Piquant Gammon

1.5 kg (3 lb) fore-
  end bacon joint
1 tablespoon oil
1 large onion,
  quartered
1 bay leaf
300 ml (½ pint)
  water
500 g (1 lb)
  potatoes, halved
500 g (1 lb) carrots,
  halved lengthways
250 g (8 oz)
  mange-tout
salt
TO FINISH (optional):
cloves
soft brown sugar
SAUCE:
1 tablespoon
  cornflour, blended
  with 3 tablespoons
  single cream
1 tablespoon chopped
  parsley
1 tablespoon green
  peppercorns

Weigh the bacon joint and calculate
the cooking time, allowing 8 minutes
per 500 g (1 lb).

Heat the oil in the pressure cooker,
add the bacon joint and brown all
over. Add the onion, bay leaf and
water.

Seal the cooker and bring to *High*
pressure. Cook for the calculated
time. Reduce the pressure quickly.

Add the vegetables and a little salt.
Seal and bring back to *High* pressure.
Cook for 4 minutes. Reduce the
pressure quickly. Transfer to a
warmed serving dish and keep
warm, discarding the bay leaf.

If wished, remove the skin from
the bacon, score the fat, stud with
cloves and sprinkle with sugar.

Pour the blended cornflour into
the cooker and bring to the boil,
stirring. Boil for 3 minutes, then stir
in the parsley and peppercorns. Serve
with the meat.

Serves 4 to 6

NOTE: If mange-tout are unavailable,
use fresh or frozen whole green beans.

Coconut and Vegetable Curry

2 large onions
5 cm (2 inch) piece
 root ginger
6 celery sticks
2 large carrots
2 young turnips
250 g (8 oz)
 courgettes
250 g (8 oz) yam or
 sweet potato
1 green chilli, deseeded
2 small green
 (pickling) mangoes
3 cloves garlic
4 tablespoons clarified
 butter (see page 40)
1 aubergine, cubed
1 teaspoon each
 ground fenugreek,
 cumin, coriander,
 turmeric, chilli,
 cardamom and
 paprika
1 × 283 g (10 oz)
 can coconut milk
 (unsweetened)
salt
TO GARNISH:
½ red pepper, cut
 into rings
chopped coriander
2 tablespoons pine nuts

Coarsely chop the onions. Slice the ginger. Cut the celery into 3.5 cm (1½ inch) lengths, the carrots into 8 pieces each, and the turnips into small segments. Cut the courgettes into 1 cm (½ inch) cubes. Slice the yam or sweet potato and chilli. Cut the mangoes into quarters and remove the stones. Chop the garlic.

Heat the butter in the pressure cooker, add the onions, ginger, garlic and aubergine and fry for 2 minutes. Stir in the celery, carrots, turnips and ground spices and cook for 1 minute. Add the remaining ingredients, with salt to taste.

Seal the cooker and bring to *High* pressure. Cook for 5 minutes. Reduce the pressure quickly.

Pour into a warmed serving dish. Arrange the pepper rings on top and sprinkle with chopped coriander and pine nuts.

Serve with a 'flat' bread, such as nan or pitta, or poppadoms.

Serves 4

NOTE: Coconut milk is available in delicatessens and Asian food stores.

Steak, Kidney and Mushroom Pudding

15 g (½ oz) butter
1 tablespoon oil
500 g (1 lb) stewing
    or braising steak,
    cut into 1.5 cm
    (¾ inch) cubes
175 g (6 oz) ox
    kidney, cut into
    1.5 cm (¾ inch)
    cubes
salt and pepper
450 ml (¾ pint) beef
    stock
175 g (6 oz) button
    mushrooms
2 tablespoons
    chopped parsley
PASTRY:
175 g (6 oz)
    self-raising flour
pinch of salt
75 g (3 oz) shredded
    suet
150 ml (¼ pint)
    water
    (approximately)

Heat the butter and oil in the pressure cooker. Add the steak, kidney, and salt and pepper to taste and fry until evenly browned. Add the stock.

Seal the cooker and bring to *High* pressure. Cook for 15 minutes. Reduce the pressure quickly. Add the mushrooms and leave for a few minutes; strain, reserving the stock.

Sift the flour and salt into a basin. Stir in the suet and enough water to make a soft dough. Knead lightly.

Roll out into a large circle, cut out a quarter in a triangular shape and reserve. Use the pastry to line a lightly greased 900 ml (1½ pint) pudding basin, overlapping the edge. Trim off any excess and roll out with the reserved pastry for the top.

Mix the parsley into the meat and put into the basin. Two-thirds fill with reserved stock. Dampen the lid and put in position, sealing well.

Cover with lightly oiled greaseproof paper and foil, making a pleat across the centre. Secure with string.

Pour 900 ml (1½ pints) boiling water and 1 teaspoon vinegar into the cleaned cooker and bring back to the boil. Put the trivet in position and stand the basin on it. Seal the cooker but do not fit the weight. When steam escapes from the centre vent, lower the heat and steam for 10 minutes.

Put on the weight and bring to *Low* pressure. Cook for 35 minutes. Reduce the pressure quickly.

Turn out the pudding onto a warmed serving dish. Reheat the reserved liquor and serve with the pudding, accompanied by sautéed courgettes.
Serves 4

MULTI-COOKER MEALS

Multi-cookers, also known as electric frying pans, are more than just temperature-controlled frying pans. Steaming, braising, roasting, baking and poaching are all possible. The large, evenly heated cooking surface makes one-pot cooking easy and they can be unplugged and used for serving, too, thus avoiding the need for a serving dish. By contrast with slow cookers, food can be browned to develop flavour and aid appearance.

Multi-cookers have a high domed cover with a vent in it so that the pan can be converted very quickly for roasting or baking with the vent open and for other cooking processes with the vent closed. Follow the individual manufacturer's instructions and directions for settings.

A wide range of one-pot meals, from the typical British Sunday lunch of roast meat and two vegetables to interesting meals without meat, can be cooked in this one appliance. Its large capacity makes it especially useful when entertaining or cooking large quantities for freezing.

Creamy Duck with Apples

2 tablespoons oil
1 large duckling, cut into 8 portions
250 g (8 oz) button onions
1 clove garlic, chopped
2 dessert apples, peeled, cored and each cut into 4 rings
salt and pepper
300 ml (½ pint) dry cider
6 juniper berries, lightly crushed
227 g (8 oz) frozen peas, thawed
4 tablespoons double cream

Heat the oil in the pan at setting 4, add the duckling portions and fry for about 5 minutes, until lightly browned, turning as necessary; remove. Add the onions and garlic and fry for 3 minutes. Replace the duckling and place an apple slice on each. Sprinkle with salt and pepper. Add the cider and juniper berries.

Cover, close the vent, turn to '1' and cook for 1 hour or until tender.

Add the peas and heat for 3 minutes with the vent open. Stir in the cream and cook with the vent open for 2 minutes.

Serve with grated carrot and celery salad.
Serves 4

Grandmother's Steamed Chicken

1 × 1.5 kg (3½ lb)
  chicken with
  giblets
salt and pepper
250 g (8 oz) button
  mushrooms
3 tablespoons
  chopped parsley
25 g (1 oz) butter
½ lemon
1.2 litres (2 pints)
  water
small bunch of mixed
  herbs
500 g (1 lb) young
  carrots
6 celery sticks,
  halved
350 g (12 oz) new
  potatoes
2 teaspoons cornflour,
  blended with
  1 tablespoon water

Sprinkle the chicken inside and out with salt and pepper. Put the mushrooms, 1 tablespoon of the parsley and the butter into the body of the bird. Place the ½ lemon in the opening to close it up.

Stand the chicken on the baking rack in the pan. Pour in the water and add the giblets and herbs. Heat at setting 5 until boiling. Lower the heat to '1', cover and close the vent. Cook for about 1½ hours or until the chicken is very tender. Add the carrots, celery and potatoes for the last 20 minutes.

Transfer the chicken to a warmed serving dish and surround with the vegetables.

Strain the stock and return 450 ml (¾ pint) to the pan. Stir in the blended cornflour and bring to the boil, stirring until thickened. Stir in the remaining parsley and serve with the chicken.

Serves 4 to 6

Turkey with Tapenade

50 g (2 oz) butter
3 tablespoons oil
125 g (4 oz) white
  bread, diced
500 g (1 lb) boneless
  cooked turkey,
  diced
2 onions, sliced
1/2 × 227 g (8 oz)
  frozen stewpack
  vegetables, thawed
6 eggs
3 tablespoons single
  cream
salt and pepper
2 tablespoons chopped
  parsley to garnish
TAPENADE:
1 clove garlic, crushed
75 g (3 oz) black
  olives, stoned and
  chopped
4 button mushrooms,
  finely chopped
2 teaspoons anchovy
  essence
2 tablespoons olive
  oil
1/4 teaspoon mixed
  herbs
pepper

First, make the tapenade. Work all the ingredients together, with pepper to taste, in a blender or food processor until smooth. Alternatively, chop the garlic, olives and mushrooms as small as possible, then stir in the anchovy essence, oil, herbs, and pepper to taste.

Heat the butter and 2 tablespoons of the oil in the pan at setting 4, add the bread and turkey and fry until the bread is crisp and golden. Remove with a slotted spoon.

Add the remaining oil, the onions and stewpack vegetables and cook, stirring, until softened.

Beat the eggs and cream together until blended. Add salt and pepper to taste and pour over the vegetables. Return the bread and turkey to the pan, pressing it down into the egg. Cook, uncovered, for about 4 minutes, lifting the sides from time to time to see when it begins to brown underneath. Cover, open the vent and cook for 2 minutes.

Spoon the tapenade on top and sprinkle with parsley. Cut into 4 pieces and serve straight from the pan with tomato and onion salad.
Serves 4

Anchovy-Studded Lamb

1.5 kg (3 lb)
  shoulder of lamb
10 anchovy fillets
10 capers
1 tablespoon oil
500 g (1 lb)
  potatoes, halved
salt and pepper
500 g (1 lb)
  courgettes, thickly
  sliced
parsley sprig to
  garnish

Make 10 deep cuts in the lamb at intervals. Roll each anchovy fillet around a caper and insert in the cuts.

Heat the oil in the pan at setting 4, add the lamb, cover and close the vent. Brown on all sides for 15 minutes, turning as necessary. Add the potatoes and salt and pepper to taste.

Lower the heat to '3' and cook for 80 minutes, turning occasionally.

Transfer the meat and potatoes to a dish and keep warm. Pour off all but 2 tablespoons of the fat. Add courgettes to pan and cook, uncovered, at '3', stirring, for 6 to 8 minutes. Transfer to the serving dish. Serve garnished with parsley.
Serves 4 to 6

Apricot Stuffed Veal

1.25 kg (2½ lb)
  rolled veal
  shoulder
2 tablespoons oil
900 ml (1½ pints)
  chicken stock
500 g (1 lb) potatoes
250 g (8 oz)
  courgettes
125 g (4 oz) pre-
  soaked apricots
STUFFING:
250 g (8 oz) dried
  apricots, chopped
grated rind of 1 lemon
125 g (4 oz) fresh
  white breadcrumbs
125 g (4 oz)
  courgettes, coarsely
  grated
salt and pepper
TO GARNISH:
chopped parsley

First make the stuffing. Mix together the chopped apricots, lemon rind, breadcrumbs, courgettes, and salt and pepper to taste.

Untie the rolled veal, spread with the stuffing, roll and tie again. Sprinkle with salt and pepper.

Heat the oil in the pan at setting 4, add the veal and cook for about 10 minutes to brown all over.

Add the stock, bring to the boil, cover and close the vent and lower the heat to '1'. Cook for 1 hour, basting occasionally.

Cut the potatoes in quarters and the courgettes in half lengthways.

Add the potatoes for the last 15 minutes and the courgettes and apricots for the last 10 minutes.

Arrange the meat and vegetables on a warmed serving dish and sprinkle with parsley. Serve the cooking liquid as a sauce.
Serves 4

Sweet and Sour Pork Ribs

1.25 kg (2½ lb)
  pork ribs
½ teaspoon meat
  tenderizer
¼ teaspoon ground
  aniseed
salt and pepper
450 ml (¾ pint)
  water
2 onions, quartered
2 carrots, quartered
4 celery sticks, halved
GLAZE:
300 ml (½ pint)
  tomato ketchup
2 teaspoons soy sauce
2 tablespoons made
  mustard
1 teaspoon ground
  aniseed
2 tablespoons plum
  jam
½ teaspoon celery
  salt
½ teaspoon garlic
  salt
2 tablespoons vinegar
2 tablespoons Worcester-
  shire sauce
TO GARNISH:
celery leaves

Place the ribs in the pan and sprinkle
with the tenderizer, aniseed, and salt
and pepper to taste. Add the water,
cover and bring to the boil at setting
5. Lower to '1', close the vent and
cook for 1 hour or until tender,
adding the onions, carrots and celery
for the last 20 minutes. Strain,
reserving the stock.

Mix together the ingredients for
the glaze, adding 3 tablespoons
reserved stock.

Return the ribs to the pan and
pour over the glaze, turning the ribs
so they are coated on both sides.
Return the vegetables, cover, close
the vent and cook at '4' for
5 minutes. Stir well, then cook for
2 to 3 minutes with the vent open,
until tender.

Garnish with celery leaves. Serve
with bean sprout and cucumber
salad.
Serves 4

Baked Stuffed Marrow

2 marrows, about
  400 g (14 oz) each
2 tablespoons oil
1 small onion, chopped
250 g (8 oz) minced
  beef
125 g (4 oz) minced
  pork
2 tablespoons
  chopped parsley
1 teaspoon
  Worcestershire
  sauce
salt and pepper
250 g (8 oz) chicken
  livers, halved
1 egg, beaten
8 prunes, stoned
4 rashers back bacon,
  derinded, halved
  and rolled
150 ml (¼ pint)
  water
1 bay leaf
25 g (1 oz) butter
parsley sprigs to
  garnish

Cut the marrows in half lengthways and remove the seeds.

Heat the oil in the pan at setting 4, add the onion, beef and pork and fry until lightly browned. Turn off the heat and add the parsley, Worcestershire sauce, and salt and pepper to taste.

Set aside 12 half livers, chop the rest and add to the pan with the egg. Mix well together and spoon into the marrow. Put a piece of chicken liver at each end and in the centre of each piece of marrow, with 2 prunes and 2 bacon rolls in between. Add the water, bay leaf and butter to the pan, then put in the marrow.

Cook at '4' until the water boils, then cover, close the vent and lower the heat to '1'. Cook for 20 minutes. Discard the bay leaf. Garnish with parsley and serve with potato salad.
Serves 4

Seafood Chaudrée

1 bottle dry white
 wine
4 cloves garlic, crushed
few parsley stalks
salt and white pepper
125 g (4 oz)
 long-grain rice
good pinch of
 powdered saffron
4 celery sticks, halved
250 g (8 oz) shelled
 broad beans
1 kg (2 lb) mixed
 white fish (e.g.
 coley, monk fish,
 whiting), cut into
 large pieces
250 g (8 oz) prawns
 in shells, tail
 shells removed
142 ml (5 fl oz)
 soured cream
1 tablespoon plain
 flour
chopped parsley to
 garnish

Put the wine, garlic, parsley stalks, and salt and pepper to taste in the pan, cover and bring to the boil at setting 5. Lower the heat to '3' and cook, uncovered, for 15 minutes to reduce the wine.

Add the rice, saffron, celery and beans and cook covered with the vent closed for 15 minutes, adding all the fish after 5 minutes. Transfer the fish and vegetables to a warmed serving dish.

Mix the cream and flour together and add to the liquid remaining in the pan. Bring to the boil, stirring, until smooth. Pour over the fish, sprinkle with parsley and serve with French bread.

Serves 4

Layered Fish Terrine

350 g (12 oz) fresh
    spinach
salt and pepper
2 carrots, thinly
    sliced
850 g (1¾ lb)
    frozen plaice
    fillets, thawed and
    skinned
lemon juice
1 × 439 g (15½ oz)
    can pink salmon,
    drained
2 egg whites
1 teaspoon tomato
    purée
1 tablespoon double
    cream
grated nutmeg
2 teaspoons chopped
    chives or spring
    onions
TO SERVE:
2-3 fennel bulbs,
    quartered
350-500 g (12 oz-
    1 lb) French beans
2-3 carrots, peeled
    downwards into
    curls

Remove the thick stems from the spinach. Wash well and place in the pan, heated at setting 5, with just the water clinging to it. Cook for 1 to 2 minutes until beginning to soften; remove.

Pour 1.2 litres (2 pints) salted water into pan, add sliced carrots and boil for 1 minute; remove.

Line the base and sides of a greased 750-900 ml (1¼-1½ pint) loaf tin with some of the spinach leaves, placing a few carrot slices between the leaves at intervals. Lay 3 or 4 plaice fillets on top, adding salt, pepper and lemon juice to taste.

Remove the skin and bones from the salmon, chop finely and mix with 1 egg white, the tomato purée, cream and salt and pepper to taste; beat well.

Chop the remaining plaice fillets and mix with the remaining egg white, adding salt and pepper to taste. Squeeze the remaining spinach dry and season with salt, pepper and nutmeg to taste.

Put two-thirds of the salmon mixture in a layer in the tin, cover with the remaining spinach and carrots. Top with two-thirds of the remaining fish fillet mixture. Stir the remaining fish mixtures together with the chives or spring onions and completely cover the top.

Cover with buttered foil and place in the water in the pan. Cover and heat at '5' until the water boils, then lower to '1' and close the vent; cook for 45 minutes. Add the fennel to the water for the last 15 minutes, the French beans for 10 minutes, and the carrots for 5 minutes.

Turn out the terrine and serve sliced, hot or cold, with mayonnaise and the drained vegetables.
Serves 4 to 6

Scallops Parisienne

250 g (8 oz)
  Jerusalem
  artichokes, sliced
227 g (8 oz) frozen,
  sliced green beans,
  thawed
salt and pepper
25 g (1 oz) butter
1 tablespoon oil
1 small onion,
  chopped
12-16 frozen scallops,
  depending on size,
  thawed
2 tablespoons plain
  flour
1 teaspoon paprika
450 ml (¾ pint) milk
TO GARNISH:
1 tablespoon chopped
  parsley
4 small tomatoes,
  halved

Put the artichokes and beans in the
pan, cover with 1.2 litres (2 pints)
boiling salted water, cover and bring
back to the boil at setting 5. Lower
the heat to '1' and cook for
12 minutes; drain.

Dry the pan, heat the butter and
oil, add the onion and sauté for 2 to
3 minutes. Stir in the scallops and
cook for 3 minutes. Add the flour
and paprika and cook, stirring, for
1 minute. Gradually add the milk,
stirring, to make a sauce.

Replace the vegetables and reheat
for 3 minutes. Sprinkle with the
parsley, garnish with the tomatoes
and serve with hot buttered toast.
Serves 4

Honey-Glazed Trout

15 g (½ oz) unsalted
   butter
2 tablespoons oil
25 g (1 oz) slivered
   almonds
2 shallots, chopped
4 celery sticks, finely
   sliced
salt and pepper
1 tablespoon plain
   flour
1½ teaspoons ground
   ginger
4 × 175 g (6 oz)
   trout, cleaned
2 tablespoons honey
6 tablespoons white
   wine
1 × 340 g (12 oz)
   can asparagus
   spears, drained

Heat the butter and oil in the pan at
setting 4, add the almonds and fry
until brown; remove with a slotted
spoon. Add the shallots, celery, and
salt and pepper to taste and fry for
3 minutes.

Season the flour with ½ teaspoon
of the ginger and use to coat the
trout. Add to the pan and fry for
1 minute on each side. Mix the
remaining ginger with the honey and
wine and pour over the trout. Add
the asparagus.

Cover, close the vent, and lower
the heat to '1'. Cook for 5 minutes,
until the asparagus is heated through
and the liquid is a glaze.

Serve with a new potato salad.

Serves 4

INDEX

Acknowledgments
Photography by James Jackson
Food prepared by Clare Ferguson
Photographic stylist: Lesley Richardson